live

bird may live as long as twenty years. Eve

bird may live as long as twenty years. Eve

Praise for Trace Ramsey's Writing

"Trace Ramsey imbues his writing with a humanity that can't be faked. He writes from a core of truth with illuminating, descriptive, deeply personal prose. If we read to learn we're not alone in our feelings, then this is a guide to understanding there are plenty of others out there who feel the same."

Bart Schaneman, author of *Someplace Else: On Wanderlust, Expatriate Life, and the Call of the Wild*

"Trace's writing is engrossingly polished, yet still brimming with spontaneous energy and ragged beauty. The writing is dense and detailed, it demands the reader's attention and full focus. It's difficult to firmly classify; it uses memory as a literary device, and it's often honest to the point of brutality."

Zine Nation

"There's a certain rare type of writing, to see beyond the obvious and easy, to fix upon the translucent forms that dance elusively about our periphery. Trace Ramsey ventures unflinchingly into the emotional landscape. Intimate and sometimes stark, he engages us by tapping a common well of humanity, and shining light into dark corners. There are no wasted words."

Jack Cheiky
Syndicated Zine Reviews

"Trace's descriptions of the nature around them and attention to detail are superb, putting the reader right into their writing, as though you're experiencing the dry grass beneath their feet, the hot summer nights in the South, and the personal family tragedy that lives in your blood and veins and travels on to your children."

Razorcake

"One thing I've always admired about Trace's writing is that he manages to look back at the past without getting sentimental about it. His stories and essays are like autopsies, laying bare what it means to be part of a family, what it's like to struggle with depression, what it's like to be alive in this world; even the tender moments aren't over-romanticized. This is the hard stuff, the raw stuff, but there's beauty here, too—the beauty that comes from describing life as it is in all its heartbreak and its glory."

Jessie Lynn McMains, author of *What We Talk About When We Talk About Punk*

"Trace Ramsey's lush prose takes the reader into a challenging space. While it often settles into the darker realms of the mind, it is also contemplative and rewarding with a message of finding purpose in living life for those we love. Ramsey's writing may find him walking alongside his demons, probing them, and conversing with them, but it is, ultimately, an uplifting look at the journey of life for those whose minds deal with mental illness on a daily basis."

Kurt Morris, author of *Fiercely Lonely*

"I believe wholeheartedly in the worth and import of Trace Ramsey's work. With his words he shows the dark heart of family and the result is troubled, devastating, and powerfully beautiful."

Adam Gnade, author of *Locust House*

"Trace takes a moment in time and illuminates something human within it—a touch, a look, a conversation and it is heart-wrenching. His writing is a reminder that we are part of something bigger than what is inside us even when it doesn't feel that way. It's an understanding that despite all of that, our internal ecosystem doesn't stop moving and growing for even one second. It's an observation on survival that is brutal and beautiful but not at all romanticized."

Sophie Ioannou
Gut Feelings Zine

all I want to do is live

A Collection of Creative Nonfiction
Trace Ramsey

Pioneers Press
100 E Kansas Ave, #248
Lansing, Kansas 66043
www.pioneerspress.com

© 2017 by Trace Ramsey
All rights reserved
Printed in the United States of America
First edition, 2017

Publisher's Cataloging-in-Publication Data

Names: Ramsey, Trace.
Title: All I want to do is live : a collection of creative nonfiction / Trace Ramsey.
Description: Lansing, KS: Pioneers Press, 2017.
Identifiers: ISBN 978-1-939899-28-6 (pbk.)
           978-1-939899-29-3 (e-book)
Subjects: LCSH: American literature--21st century. | Creative nonfiction. | Essays. | Poetry. | Autobiography. | BISAC: LITERARY COLLECTIONS / American / General.| BIOGRAPHY & AUTOBIOGRAPHY / Personal Memoirs.
Classification: LCC PS3618.A4786 A45 2017 (print) | LCC PS3618.A4786 (e-book) | DDC 818/.6--dc23.

Library of Congress Control Number: 2016962700

WWW.ALLIWANTTODOISLIVE.COM
WWW.PATREON.COM/QUITTER

Acknowledgments

Farthing Street first appeared in *At Length Magazine*
Briggs Avenue first appeared in *Hippocampus Magazine*
Viscera first appeared in *concis*
You and I first appeared in *I Don't Know How to Help You*

Author image courtesy of Fábio Vermelho

Interviews used with permission from *Gut Feelings Zine* and J. David Osborne

The image of a South African griffin vulture (*Gyps coprotheres*) was adapted from *The Hunter's Arcadia* by Parker Gillmore, published in 1886 by Chapman & Hall. All text and images from *The Hunter's Arcadia* are in the public domain.

Contents

Part One: Nonfiction Chapbooks & Zines

Quitter #7 *(2013)* 16
Quitter #8 *(2014)* 38
Quitter #9 *(2015)* 54
Fog Index #1 *(2015)* 76
Quitter #10 *(2016)* 91

Part Two: Poetry Chapbooks

Gravity Kills #1 *(2011)* 119
Gravity Kills #2 *(2017)* 129

Part Three: Essays and Flash Nonfiction

Briggs Avenue 143
Thin 153
Viscera 155
You & I 157
Hot & Cold 160
Blood Moon 163
Blur 165
Farthing Street 169

Part Four: Interviews

Trace Ramsey's Brain Map 189
An Interview with J. David Osborne . . . 198

all I want
to do is live

Introduction

As the forested mountains of North Carolina burn hundreds of miles away, the particulates and the haze travel east. My two children and I are on the porch when the worst of it comes through. The smell is nothing like a campfire. There is something else in the smoke, some other ingredient that identifies the lives the fire has ruined or taken. On the porch, in the premature descent into evening, we imitate the rumbling and frightening noise of a mass of black vultures. We giggle, all of us, as our growls become a joke, our vibrating throats a source of light. How else to explain tragedy in a way that a four-year-old and a one-year-old might accept and understand? They do not need the weight of truth. They deserve to be children, to gather the dark things slowly, to not have to ache. I must always remind myself that behind the fires comes rebirth; below the vultures, new life. These kids are my new life, life that has the possibility of freedom from what afflicts me.

What does it mean for me to live, to say a thing like *all I want to do is live*? It is a question that I do not know how to analyze because it is a question that—for me—gives changing answers. For people like me who deal with sometimes debilitating depression and anxiety and addiction, a desire to *not live* can become very powerful and attractive. It is as if the body is full of iron filings and death is a massive magnet. But how to get away from that pull, to repel it, to feel needed as a source of strength when there is nothing of the sort within you?

Late that night I collapse into bed, the fire still in my nose, my cheeks tight from laughing. In that moment, I am content and thinking of strange things like the useful insides of a broken clock and the cheese and scallion sandwiches that my grandfather used to make and honeysuckle vines full of dark orange flowers shaped like baby trombones. I like to hang my stories in the closets of rooms I slept in once, just a game of association that connects missing physical representations of memory to empty wine bottles on a curb, old stringy blood, prom nights I spent at work instead of on the dance floor.

There is a path through it, this illness that may seem to saturate what you are about to read. Maybe you'll see something here that makes you feel like you are not alone or something that makes you understand a close friend or partner. We want to live, and we want to live with you.

Trace
Durham, NC
February 2017

For Pinwheel

Part One:
Nonfiction Chapbooks & Zines

I wish I could say that it was surreal the first time I butchered an animal.

Quitter #7

It was not; it was rote, mechanical, genetic, practical. A rabbit wedged in the crotch of a tree branch, my five fingers prehensile around a knife, pulling the innards out slowly, rather unsure yet determined. I made no prehistoric grunts, just internal nods at the recognition of biology, that we beings are surely all built the same way, one long branching tube from mouth to asshole providing the physical and chemical mechanics of life; the chicken the same as the ox only smaller, the ape the same as the roach but larger.

It was early Winter. I was panting from running and following the screaming beagles as they chased on the dispersing scent of the rabbit. The dogs howled as they ran on and on, continuously circling away from me then toward me, a sloppy swing of quick cuts and almost undetectable stops, their cold galloping feet tracing lines in the snow throughout the low forest. I fired once at the rabbit as it crossed to my side, bird-shot screeching from the gun barrel and through some brambles. The ear ringing mark of a single shotgun shell echoed among the striped maples and red oaks, long cleared of leaves. I ejected the shell from the gun and took in the sweet metallic whisper of it. I was ten years old, sniffling from the cold air cracking my mouth and nostrils, looking quietly at a lump of brownish gray fur that no longer moved. My step-father stood over me pointing and pushing instructions on me.

The fur of the rabbit came off quickly, small fibers of connective tissue making a wet noise not unlike the crinkling cellophane of a return envelope. I cut small rings around each foot, first through the fur and then through the joints joining the bones, snapping each paw off and letting them dangle like grapes on a vine. The final cut severed the head from the body. All but the meat was left in a pile on the ground, the heat of the guts melting a small riddle of ridges in the snow allowing the heap to sink at different speeds to the frozen earth below. The guts and tiny head—with its dark, half closed eyes—looked like a mask resting on pink and brown snakes, unmoving as the curtain dropped on a macabre play performed for the crows.

I didn't say any prayers at the butchering. I didn't offer any thanks to the rabbit. I didn't think I needed to, really. It was just a rabbit, simply a rabbit, only a rabbit, as I was told by my stepfather that it was just and simply and only a rabbit. I would come to realize, far in the future and away from this gray forest, that he was always incapable of sympathy or thinking beyond his own skull.

He was a crowing man, given to expanding himself into where he never was, claiming credit for things he barely understood. He was also a cruel man, a barbarian in a yawning sense of the word, ready to raise his voice and hands against anyone smaller or weaker than himself. This is the same man who kicked my brother in the stomach for forgetting to flush the toilet; the same man who threw me up the set of concrete steps outside our home for raking the leaves incorrectly; the same man who left bruises the size of oranges just below my mother's elbows from where he would grab her and force her to listen to every. last. word.

At dinner, my mother would ruin the rabbit. She would bake it in cheap, overly sweet tomato sauce. There was always too much onion. The result was an acidic, chewy meat served without additions – no potatoes, no bread and certainly no rice. There would be periodic murmured exclamations around the table as someone would bite into a pellet from the killing shell.

The only talking came from the tiny speaker of the thirteen inch television perched on the kitchen counter. The television was always on at dinner, providing context and detail of a world outside the door of our double wide. It was on that television that I followed the Reagan presidency, learned of school closings due to snow and heard that Stevie Ray Vaughan had died in a helicopter accident.

The silence around the table was built by my stepfather. If he wasn't talking then there is no way you were. And that was the end of it. There was never any discussion about what was learned in school or how work went or what we might do over the weekend. There was nothing to indicate an existence as a family beyond all of us sitting around a table wishing we never brought this rabbit home.

November

I grew up knowing that come November there would be a deer hanging somewhere in the front yard, probably by the antlers or the neck and probably from the branch of a tree. Or maybe hanging out of the bed of the pickup truck. Or from a rafter in the dirt floor garage.

I knew that the stories of how that *"big buck"* came to be dead would be floating around the house until they could be recited, with all the groan inducing embellishments, by people in the house who could say nothing in return. This was my stepfather's personal mythology, another way to blanket us with his control. I could probably dig deep enough to remember one or two of those stories, but who gives a shit really?

My maternal grandfather also told stories, the ones that I have not forgotten on purpose, the ones about how the deer tricked him or showed him up or maybe never even existed. The stories always began with my grandfather sitting on a stump, watching his breath leave his face and disperse. There would be a cracking sound, a stick snapping close by. He would stop breathing, close his eyes, crank all possible processing power to his ears. He would triangulate, check his heartbeat and turn his head only to see nothing but the cold of a Fall morning staring back at him. He would smile at us, the story clearly ending there. He could provide lessons without lecturing, saying *"you will be fooled, but don't take it personally"*.

He never gave in to my stepfather's superficial glory of shooting something in the face; when a deer was in the freezer before December my grandfather seemed satisfied with the knowledge that, with the deer's help, he and his family would have food for the winter. He didn't amuse in the winners and losers of what most sane people would see as a wholly lopsided conflict heavily subsidized by civilization and its tools—a heavily armed human against an unprepared, unwilling and unaware opponent.

My grandfather's task was brutal regardless, but maybe less so as there were no mounted heads on the walls of his home like there were in our home. The need for those stuffed and preserved reminders is something that I couldn't explain back then, but know now is an indication of small mindedness, a dedication to the outward projection of dominance when you know that you are inescapably weak inside. You are a collector with no sense of how to interact with the

dead or the living, both phases of life simply reminders of inadequacy, weak interpersonal skills and low self-esteem. If you have a deer head or a stuffed fish on your wall, go look at it and ask yourself what reminder it serves that could not otherwise be captured by a photograph or poem. Is it there to show your friends and family what a fucking hero you are?

When I was twenty, I volunteered twice to travel with a New York DEC deer ager on their rounds. For fourteen hours we visited deer processing places as well as any house that had a deer hanging in the front yard. My job was to write while the ager examined teeth and called out the ages of each dead deer.

I think it was during this time that I became permanently desensitized to the sights and smells of dead non-human animals. At each processor were dozens of barrels and drums and tarps full of various parts; piles of legs next to buckets of guts and tails; lines of deer carcasses waiting to be disassembled by hacksaws, band saws and reciprocating saws, mostly frozen in rigor mortis or by the depth of cold in the evening air. Steam escaped from some of the recent arrivals, a sign that they were less than an hour dead.

There can be nothing more brutal or common or necessary than taking a life in order to eat and sustain a body. Non-human animals do it without question, without any perceptible remorse or hesitation. What makes our actions so much different?

We pull carrots from the soil, ending their run with gravity, ending their gathering of sugar and all the processes that made them a living thing. They may not scream or run or struggle much, but a carrot is a living thing nonetheless and we must kill it in order to eat it.

Eating a carrot is nothing like eating an animal, which is why many choose not to eat the latter at all. I respect that choice; it was a choice that I had once made as well. As with eating it, killing a carrot is nothing like killing an animal. Animals articulate their disappointment in our choice to kill them in blood gurgles, screams and the twitches of ending nerve impulses. We destroy them in order that we can live; we destroy them for other reasons as well, reasons that have no bearing on survival. If you do not believe that then you deny that your meal had any previous life beyond its packaging. I apologize, but I can't let you do that.

July

My father taught me how to swim by lobbing me into the middle of a pool. He would throw me; I would splash in, quickly return to the surface and begin to flail around. Between spitting and gasping I would reach for the side of the pool, basically learning to swim by lunging in the direction of the closest solid object. When I reached an edge, my father would lift me out of the water by the arms, my smooth torso brushing against the hair of his shirtless chest. I would get a whiff of his breath—a punch of pilsner, a pinch of bourbon—just before he threw me back in. Splash in, return to the surface, and seek stability; life lessons roiling and foaming in 22,000 gallons of chlorine and algaecide.

This process continued, on and on as other children played in the water and their mothers lay on the deck on their bellies, their bikini tops untied, canned beers sweating beside their browning shoulders. No matter which side of the pool I would reach, my father would be there to pluck me from the water and toss me back out to the middle. Sometimes he would pause to jump in the pool himself, get his cut-off jean shorts soaked and later ask the sun to dry them as he went back to educating his child.

Of course nothing bad was going to happen to me. I was bounded by giggling adults and larger children, all well aware of the lesson I was receiving. This is the way my father learned. *(I was told that my paternal grandfather learned by falling into an open well.)* This method was apparently the only proper way for a boy my age to *"understand"* the nature of swimming and its physics, a way for me to conquer the water for myself and take it as dominion. I can imagine my grandfather speaking of dominion as he repeatedly tossed my father into a pond from the edges of a boat dock. Dominion then may have been in a different context, a context of control over the minds and actions of your child, rather than that of a global lesson about viscosity and drag.

I imagine that the fear my father had once clenched in his stomach had grown old and rusty if not nostalgic, a flowered, withered and decomposed bit of experience with no current equivalent in his life. His father was dead. He no longer sought out the weaknesses in their relationship or thought that his swimming education was anything more than playful fun. It was most likely an abusive lesson just as mine was, if only temporary instead of some other long-term sorts of abuses. I guess it would be much as the childhood pain of slamming your hand in a car door tends to fully dissipate by the age of twenty.

A few years after my lessons, it was time for my brother to learn. By this time I was able to participate in the instruction, but the most I could do was laugh at how foolish he looked, how his small, bright hands slapped the water all around him, the splashes jostling various inflated pool toys around on tiny bubbly waves. Gone were my own thoughts on how much pain I felt from gulping water, how embarrassed I felt for crying and screaming, how much revenge I craved as my cold-blooded brain switched on. My brother was helpless just like I was, his face contorted into a weird crying smirk.

When we were kids, all my friends and I knew when my brother had to take a shit. He got that same skewered smirk on his face, crossing his legs at his feet, arms limp at his sides as if he were sleeping upright. He would stand in that position until the waves of peristalsis ceased for a bit and he could comfortably throw the baseball or go hiking or whatever it was we were doing at the time. My brother always denied the reasons for the time-outs and glossy eyes. But we could all take one look and know that gravity was working on his colon, the waste in his system burrowing to freedom.

When he was nineteen, my brother jumped from the roof of a four story building, breaking most of the breakable parts of his body. His bones shattered into multiple pieces, nerve endings and memories erased forever. He had shit himself, but he was salvageable. He found out that you cannot learn how to fly the same way you learn how to swim.

A person is not like a twig or an egg shell. We mostly have the ability to mend and accept that mending in a permanent way. Sometimes the need for mending is mental and hidden from the people who fix these things. In those cases we jump. In those cases we need to jump, to hide ourselves in the quickly approaching pavement, become a part of its blackness, its impervious memory.

September

I remember it was sometime in the Fall; all day long the cool air dried my throat on its way in, the same air emerging warm and humid, personal clouds of breath falling up and away into the surrounding atmosphere. At the time I was in Western New York. That particular atmosphere was most likely gray and barely concealing the threat of snow or sleet. It was too early for snow, if I recall correctly, even for this small town sandwiched between Lakes Ontario and Erie and its lake effects.

Fallen leaves blew into the street, crashing and skittering into each other like poorly made airplanes. Against that threatening gray sky the variant colors of leaves haloed the random limbs of the nearly empty trees, the branches narrowing to the twigs at the extremities, each little wooden finger moving crisply with the air movements above. From minute to minute these trees are safely bolted to the ground by a thickened trunk and miles of root hairs and fungal partnerships, their leaves safe to depart without harming its own life.

Beginnings and ends are buried in this particular color contrast; browns and reds fidgeting against the dirty white background above us, those few hopeful, final leaves holding on to that last stage of senescence just long enough to end up right on the top of the pile, the last to land, the last to decay. With the passing hours and minutes, the leaf layer forms on the lawns and the curbs and the shrubbery of the immediate world, not only a beginning but an end point in a constant cycle.

So what am I remembering exactly? The time I am thinking of is just like any other from that point in my life—

awake to the boredom of youth, brush against the boredom of family during breakfast. Get on a school bus full of variable stressors and hassles, depart and navigate the hallways and school lunch table seating. Become obsessed with vaguely defined friendships, sexual frustration and the confused and bullying tastes of peer pressure. The cycle is repeated in reverse, the bus empties me at home, the television comes on and the disaster of teenage life hides itself in the couch cushions or the sheets of an unmade bed.

When I was a teen, there were moments in which I laid in bed for an entire day, stomach down, face toward the wall. I was immobile, pushed into the mattress by a compression of something outside of my control, something I did not understand. Breath came short and shallow, the room dark enough to give shadows very little running room into the corners. The sheets on the bed warmed rapidly and cooled slowly, crumpled in the middle and taut at the corners, stagnant under my weight and despite my darting thoughts. I felt like a leaf caught in the bushes.

When you are young, you can't assign a name to it, this thing, this *"depression"*. You think it is just a part of life, something that comes along with breathing and aging and carrying a heavy mammal brain. Left untreated the first bout of depression will usually lead to another several years down the road. From there the half-life continues to decrease until a handful of minutes is all that stands between the dawn and the dusk of a depressive episode. For me, I am old enough now that there are no longer horizons on which to seek shelter. It just comes on, a quickly spreading net of thoughts and inaction. There is no refuge, no chance to turn it back. It just comes.

My depression shows up and opens all my doors and windows to the elements—rain, wind, sun, volcanoes, earthquakes. I am forced to greet all of it, begrudgingly welcome all the things I have no interest in revisiting—Oh hey, remember when I punched that parking meter because I got rejected by some girl at a party? Remember when that kid threw my sneakers on the roof of the school?

There isn't anything particularly emotional about what I feel, just a low energy custody of despair and sullenness, a cold thin soup of presence. My sighs become autonomic; I chew my teeth and vibrate my fingers imperceptibly. I lose words, become silent as a conservation of energy, stare at things as if they hold me upright in doing so.

I become a ghost unsure of my manner of haunting.

Depression can be like a frost; unpredictable, furious, disappointing. There is hope that neither will come at a bad time, a time where something is needed that cannot be disrupted, a time containing plans for the future and a singular requirement for growth. A flower, like a healthy mind, brings a promise of fruit.

May

My first name is rumored to have a basis in a tool known as the oscilloscope, a small bench-top machine that measures the wave shape of electrical signals. The lines appearing on the screen of the oscilloscope are referred to as the *"traces"*, usually just one but up to several lines on a basic X,Y divided axis. When I was a kid my brother and I would mess around with our father's oscilloscope, try to get the lines to make crazy shapes or pretend we were in a space capsule and the lines were voice transmissions from beyond some moon. We did not understand what the oscilloscope's purpose was other than to make a bunch of squiggles on the screen when you fiddled with the knobs. And that was enough for us at the time.

We always found the oscilloscope in the middle of the workbench in my father's shop, a small room in the corner of the enclosed breezeway dividing the house from the garage. The shop was heated, so we spent a lot of our Wintertime in there watching my father take things apart, fix something or put some piece of what-not back together. Sometimes we would help melt the solder from a variety of electronic boards and separate the capacitors and resistors into little drawers. If I close my eyes long enough and think about it, I could probably remember what the color codes on the resistors meant. We had to memorize it since we had to put the resistors in the correct drawer and couldn't ask him every time we had to file each little piece away.

The shop was always full of disassembled VCRs, ancient game systems, black and white televisions, telephones, cable boxes, kitchen appliances. If you could plug it into a wall socket, it could be found in the shop—and usually in several different pieces. Later into our teenage and young adult years, the shop was where we would go to smoke cigarettes, drink Dad's beer and make copies of rented movies. To all of the piles of assorted electronics, those new uses added quite a few half-full ashtrays, stacks of unlabeled video tapes and cardboard cases full of empty beer cans. The whole shop was a constant mess, a study in theoretical physics, evolution and decomposition, all in real time, all occurring only because of our existence there and our horrible habits, all ignored because of little green strings tracing across a screen.

String theory is the idea that electrons and other particles within an atom are not dots revolving around a nucleus but rather oscillating lines. In the field of theoretical physics, there are five major string theories, each one attempting to form an elusive Theory of Everything, a single mathematical formula to describe the physical interactions of the entire universe. But only this particular universe, since string theory also opens up the possibility of the mulitverse, layer upon layer of variant universes all with their own laws of physics.

The gap between Einstein's general relativity and modern physicists' quantum mechanics cannot be bridged without an entirely new theoretical construction. Researchers and theorists get close, discover that they need to construct another theoretical dimension or smaller particle that has a possibility of actually being observed in a real life experiment. They then test the new theory and move from there. What we can write about in a few pages of text require decades of experiments, new hypotheses, emerging talent from the university systems. Basically the five different string theories end up as untestable within any of our own sense of the word *"test"*.

Is it at all possible to violate the second law of thermodynamics, the one that says that disorder can never decrease but only come to an uneasy and most likely temporary equilibrium? Disorder can never be reversed *(says the law)*; work is always undone. Any momentum towards disorder is natural, adequate in purpose, sometimes easy to see, like a laundry hamper filling with dirty socks. You may clean the socks once the bag is full but you must always introduce work and calories and heat in order to do so. Yet the socks end up back in the hamper, a bit more worn than they were previously, just as the feet they were on are a bit more worn as well. There are no solutions to avoid the eventual disorder of the socks. Simply letting them be, letting them sit completely still on the top shelf of a closet, even keeping them sealed up in the packaging they came in, does nothing but add infinitesimally small amounts of time to the universes' plan to make those bound threads and space-age polymers into random scatters of particles.

Our own natural equilibrium most likely occurs as billions of free range molecules in the air, water and soil, not as the pliable warm flesh we are accustomed to. It is the whole mythology of *"dust to dust"* backed up by centuries of true observation as well as various thought experiments. My name, the shop in the breezeway, the oscilloscope – all temporary formations of matter and minutia studied with head scratching and dreams, the calculations drawn on chalk boards here and there, populating the archeology of our dim understanding of time and its infinite patience. Are we ourselves neither strings nor particles, rather just random assemblies of physical actions, chemical reactions and hypotheses about which cupboard holds the plates in a stranger's house?

August

It is hard for me to describe the smell or sounds of rain. It is one of those scents that leads my brain in all sorts of leaps and skips and stops—cold mornings on the cusp of April, a light rain working to break up soil for new seeds; the quick shuffle of a city street, legs and car horns and black umbrellas singing as a mass under a stinging summer downpour; a tin roof under the pounce of a quick midnight thunderstorm, pinging and ringing and whistling, directionless, soothing. Hitting an asphalt shingle, rain has the swish and dribble of water circling a drain. On a metal garbage can lid, thick droplets are like a tire iron tapping a light post, singing up and down my ear canals, membranes vibrating like a plucked guitar string.

To me, the rain scent has it all: fallen leaves and dog hair, crushed acorns and root beer soda, unadorned armpits and fresh cut mint. There are only certain other smells with this sort of ambiguity to them—the air in a deflating bicycle tire, the blood of newly pulled tooth—and those smells contain their own piece of genetic code within us, the ability to unzip a thought at the cellular level and make our reactions seem innate. If it were not for the ability of these smells to grab us and throw us into memories, we might not stand apart from the others as conscious beings. Stuck with nothing but this exact present and the slowly unfurling future, no past at all to lean on or learn from, we would be burdened with these ten fingers and ten toes, wondering why they are able to do the things that they do.

To the ear, rain is just as complex. A rolling thunderstorm sometimes hurries me back to when I was five or six years old, barely tall enough for most everything, fingers tightening on a window sash, knuckles whitening trying to pull my eyes up to the glass. Fast outlines of trees vibrated against my retinas promptly followed by low rumbles shaking the panes, always mildly enough to leave them intact —both eyes and glass—but ambitious enough to produce a reaction among all the bones of the window. Thunder and lightning were always something I would wake up for and watch until completion, the drifting storm dissolving the time between dreams into a short series of intermissions.

Among the other senses, I unfortunately do not frequently get involved in the memories of sight. I indulge them fully when I can, but vision can too easily betray a person. Heat waves floating from a sun baked highway are

really nothing tangible, as real as wind but nothing to hold onto or brace against. But those tingling apparitions bring me back to summers working in fields of cabbage, the heat rising from between the open rows, reflecting the misery of the heat of an August mid-day. The fields are open as far as you can see, fence rows barely tucking in the edges of peripheral vision. The stretches of green, watery calories—bound for harvest, for trucks, for bags, for shelves, for plates, for bellies—sit in perfect rows, silent and still except for an occasional drop of hot summer rain running down into the outer wrapper leaves.

Tonight's rain is one of those hot rains, the type that does nothing to lower the humidity or remove the stickiness from arms and foreheads. *"A warm front"*, the radio whispers as the wind picks up, a warm front moving into an already miserably warm climate. I currently live in a place where the first showers of a mid-summer front evaporate lazily from dark back roads, rising only occasionally as a vehicle parts the sick misty clouds. The next shower brings more of the same, saturating the air to the point of choking. If you have spent time in the South you know about this air. It is the kind of air that curls the covers of paperback books and makes envelopes stick together.

In this weather there is no choice but to sit six inches from a box fan, crank it to the fastest and highest settings, sit still and wait it out. There is no relief, no counter to this air thick with the grease and the swamp and the drench of another day in the Piedmont. Sweat—condensing on eyebrows, lip tops and knee pits—is not optional; it is a prerequisite for this course in human temperament. How you handle this details how you handle other personal tortures like hemorrhoids, ingrown nails and expired license plates. Our bodies are constant chain reactions of glop, responding to stimuli and adjusting internal temperature to fit the demands of any current surroundings. Cold? Get a blanket. Hot? Take off your pants.

The senses you own are your broken and rusty weapons in the war on distorted memories; how powerful or sharp or loaded with ammunition can they be if the past becomes so hazy that you forget how you wielded them or don't even care? Everything you see or taste or smell is a trick on your future memory. It will never come back in its full context, its undiluted reason. Was I really there? Did I really say that? It sounds familiar, but...

We are at the mercy of our imperfect biological and chemical functions. We do not know, truly, where we stand in the past. It is somehow vacant and arbitrary and misaligned. It is a distortion no matter how much you think it is the truth. It is only the truth now, really, in this present when all the correct gases fill the lungs, all the correct fluids irrigate the eyes. This is it; the truth as it is in the now, the next, the markings on the rain gauge.

We are not like dogs, relying on all of our senses for identification. We humans need clocks and compasses, measuring tapes and thermometers, bifocal glasses and star charts. Our instincts and innate habits are no longer there for us to lean on in a pinch. They have been bred out of us by too much time in moving vehicles, too much time spent in inebriated states, too much time contemplating broken hearts.

The heart, yes, it breaks. We feel it, but we know, scientifically, every emotion is simply an expression of the chemical mills of the brain and the guts. But we also know that any out of the ordinary input into those brains and guts can and will be processed into some staggering physical troubles. You get sick, you don't eat, you don't sleep, you dwell on the possibilities and wish you could rewind every moment in order to find out what it was that made the error get as far as your current reality. You stumble in from the rain, throwing and crumpling clothing here and there between the walls, soaked from the eyelids to the toenails, defeated from it.

Your heart, it breaks.

"I observed a huge creature walking after them in the sea."

i am there
   you are here

quitter #8
trace ramsey

Prologue

When my child Tennessee was an infant, I often carried her stomach down on my forearm. This was her favorite place to be, her calming spot. I would hold her like a football and walk through the house to settle her or get her to sleep. I made up a special song to sing to her:

> *Tennessee was a big pig*
> *had a little tail*
> *jumped over the fence*
> *went over the fence*
> *came to eat our breakfast*

Mid-summer and the rain approaches without much warning.

The wind comes up first, sucks a bit of the humidity from the air, cools things down. It is only late afternoon, but the streetlights pop on after the first heavy clouds move in to drape the sky. Traffic outside calms then disappears as the rain falls fast, a gray curtain. The rain is thick. It hangs like rope connecting soil and sky, makes seeing the house across the street nearly impossible. We sit in the living room, each of us watching the storm in our own way.

Lightning runs along a tree down the street. The strike wasn't terribly close; I couldn't hear that particular crackle. But the thunder comes right on top of the flash. It is loud like a train passing through the house. The cats scatter, their nails digging into the wood floor as best they can. The house shakes, dishes vibrate in the stainless steel sink. Tennessee drops the book she was looking at and runs to me. I sit in the rocking chair, looking out onto the street. We were all talking about the amount of water coming off the roof until right up to jolt, how we couldn't wait until the new gutters and roof got installed. Tennessee hugs my neck tight and the three of us go silent. The rest of the storm moves through quickly, all the thunder becoming distant and muted.

Post-storm yellow light enters the house. Raindrops along the edges of the storm windows invert the world and become tiny depictions of reflected reality. I watch as that pale and bright yellow gives way to dull green and eventually to the purple of an urban evening. The street lights stay on, hold the night off, hold us all in, scared of what can reach us out in the darkness. Ten gets down from my lap, grabs one of her stuffed animals and wraps it in a small blanket. She talks to it as she carries it from her mother to me and back again.

Tennessee goes still as she leans against the couch where Kristin sits. *"You lost your baby, Mama?"*

Kristin looks at me while she answers, without hesitation or sigh, *"Yes sweet'ums. But someday there may be another one."*

* * * * *

The morning after the storm, I look out the divided window of our back door. A taut wire clothesline runs parallel to my stare. The pins clasp the wire, empty. The pins are aging out there in the elements, darkening, staining with a subtly fragrant mildew. I count them slowly and silently, try to take as much time as I can spare. The green plastic coating of the wire is wet with dew, small drops of moisture form like pimples along its length. I get distracted. I start over with the counting. Once, twice; I stop only when I get the same count three times in a row. This is as close as I come to meditation. It isn't working.

Grackles move around the pokeweed that grows thick near the fence line. The birds' greasy metallic backs and tails always look wet and slick liked waxed fruit. They squeak and whistle amongst each other as I open the back door. They quickly fly off, pulling their grouping back together somewhere farther down the street. Other birds stay and watch me—a fledgling mockingbird clings to the top rung of the fence. It is guarded and fattened by each of its parents, one of them feeding the child while the other yells at me. The yelling bird spreads its wings in a threat that means nothing to me.

I slap my face hard. One slap, three slaps, no use counting just hit me; smack it out through the follicles of a numb face. Even this physical method doesn't work. Can I even explain what this is like, this understanding that gloom is coming, and there is nothing that can stop it? I am lightning connecting with a transformer on a pole; I am a race horse that just broke its leg. There is no stopping what has happened from linking with what will happen. I am entering a depressive event. I count the clothespins for a fourth time and force myself to know that I am loved, that this disease can surface from time to time and I can get through it with just that knowledge.

A chain link fence squares off our backyard. Sections of the fence are buckled from old injuries, indentations from where tree branches fell and snapped in pieces. The branches are gone, long gone. A young, thin pecan tree rises near the edge of the fence. Several of its branch tips are covered in the gray tents of webworms. Hundreds of orange headed worms will eventually drop to the ground to pupate in the fall. White moths will rise from the leaf cover and proceed with a life cycle that is easily observed. When we were kids, my brother and I would spray the lower tents with hairspray and light it all on fire. The worms would smoke and wiggle and pop in the flames. They would plunge to the ground like burning rain, and we would stomp them thoroughly like there was nothing else to do.

Tennessee and I trot out into the yard. A children's moon rests over our shoulders, a gray and flat disk passing in and out of the valleys of a few mountainous clouds. The sky is otherwise light and pale blue, reassuring. We come out back because as I stood at the door slapping myself, Tennessee came up behind me and made a fuss about wanting to pee in the yard. She really enjoys that feral and uninhibited letting go. We have no problem with her doing it. We just want her to do it in the backyard.

"Ten, you can't pee in the front yard right now. You have to wait until after the complete collapse of society makes it acceptable to pee in the front yard."

"You promise?"

"I promise. Until then, only in the backyard."

I was raised in the country and could piss wherever I wanted. My father was the lead to follow in this regard. The feeling of relieving yourself outside is something that never gets old. Whenever I visit his house, I piss on the barn just like I did as a kid.

After my parents split up, I lived with my mother and brother on a busy road near town. We only lived there for a short period of time. It was a stopover for us, a cheap duplex with cable television and bunk beds. The busy road did not deter me from pissing outside. One morning as I peed on the cement blocks of the foundation underneath the kitchen window, I looked up to see my mother and her new boyfriend looking down at me, both faces furrowed deep with anger. *"What's the big deal?"* , was all I could think to say. After I went inside and when my mother wasn't looking, her boyfriend *(my future stepfather)* hit me hard on the back of the head.

* * * * *

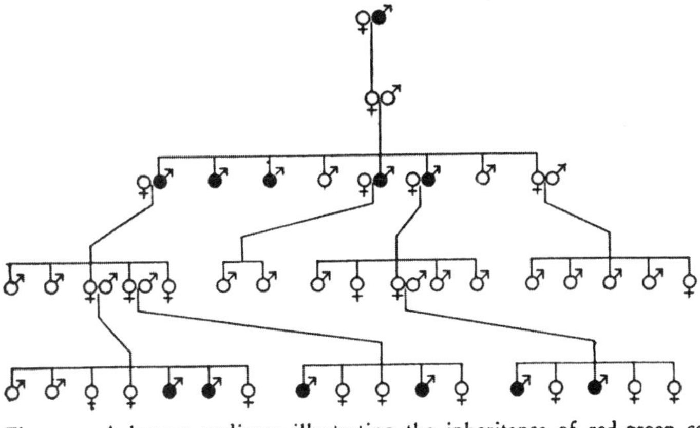

Fig. 10.—A human pedigree illustrating the inheritance of red-green color-blindness. The black circles represent affected individuals.

Tennessee digs her fingernails into the green outer hull of a pecan that fell from our tree before the nut was ready. After ten minutes of scraping the edges and tips of the hull, her fingers and palms have turned a sickly yellow. She holds her right hand to my ear because she has discovered that her sticky hand makes a slight noise as she unfurls her fist. I take her hand gently and look it over. The space under the tips of her nails is stained black like she has done nothing with her time on this planet other than dig barehanded in thick, rich soil. The lines of her palm are darker than the rest, the crevices of the folds holding harder to the stain. I take her hand in mine, ball her fist within my fist and press it all to my forehead. I close my eyes and imagine I am connecting to the ground through my child, imagining I can somehow travel through her and bury the coming sickness underground among the roots and the larvae and the constant dampness.

"Can you step on this, Papa?" She asks me to crush a pecan under the heel of my shoe. I comply. She fetches more. A greasy wet streak forms where I press my weight down on each nut, breaking it into the concrete patio. The smell as the unripe nuts come apart is strong and green like raw firewood. Tennessee keeps the pecans coming, and I keep crushing them until the concrete is frothy with the natural oil and water that emerges from the seeds.

A small pile of nut meat and sharp shell fragments builds on the patio. I tell her I am done crushing for now, that I just want to sit here and look out into the fence line and try to breathe deeply and correctly, sort myself out as my vision continues to narrow. But she doesn't understand how to stop moving, how to stop learning and receiving information, how to just take the material and sort it into neat stacks of knowledge. She convinces me to stand up from the chair to look closely at what we have done together. I find it ugly and gross. Tennessee puts her hands into the pile as if she has just discovered her meaning in life.

A squirrel runs up the tree behind us and out into the branches high above. The scratch of claws on bark is unmistakable. The squawk that follows as the creature calls out warnings to its peers is also distinct. Leaves fall as the animal crosses the expanse and jumps to another tree. I swear at the squirrel under my breath for no reason other than it seems like the sensible thing to do. These are the weird and brief moments when I think I can still mitigate and challenge what is happening by deflection and self-control.

"Do you hear that squirrel, Ten?"

"What's that squirrel saying, Papa?"

"I don't know. It seems unhappy with something, maybe unhappy with us."

The squirrel's noise stops. There is a temporary silence as we kick and throw the nut pieces out into the grass below the clothesline. By evening all the good pieces will be gone as the critters come out and lay claims among the clover and wiregrass of the yard. The mice and the birds and the opossum all have their moments when they are alone and can appreciate all this smashing I did with the heel of my foot.

A block away, the siren of a fire truck starts up and all the neighborhood dogs begin to howl along. Tennessee giggles. I focus on the dogs' reactions without thinking of the tragedy beyond the siren – the highway accident, the house on fire, the body in the street. My emotional connections are rerouted to dead ends. I breathe lazily through my partially open mouth and just stare at the ugly, rusting, and intertwined diamonds of the chain-link fence.

Tennessee hugs my leg again, and I feel nothing, shake her off. Petty and unreasonable irritation builds. I sigh hard, groan harder, grab my face with both hands and push up from chin to temple over and over again. The sound of my rough hands on the stubble of my face is sharp and familiar, but it isn't familiar enough to ground me. I am in too deep this time; there is nothing more for me to do than go lie down and sleep through the worst of it, rise in the morning and continue taking the medications that make these instances short lived.

*****

Tennessee wakes from a bad dream and can't put her words together to explain what went wrong. Her cries wake us. Kristin and I roll over to face her and calm her in the darkness of the room. We try the usual lines: *"Everything is okay, sweet one. Mama and Papa are right here. What's wrong, sweet'ums?"*, but there is nothing we can offer her except diversion. I sleepily ask her about a book we were reading before bedtime and she instantly becomes silent and then talkative. *"The bears were on wheels, Papa! What were those bears all about?"* We talk it out for a few minutes and she is calm and yawning and welcoming the pillow as she lies back down. I am jealous and wishing I was so easily distracted and mollified.

I can't go back to sleep. I think about the dream I just had where Tennessee saw my long dead grandfather Ramsey. He had a line of children, grandchildren and great-grandchildren all waiting in a line to see him and meet him as he sat still on a couch. Everyone was crying, myself included. It was that hard and cathartic dream sobbing that I have sometimes. It was a chance for me to just dump sadness like a heavy bucket of water that had no place to go, no growing tree to nourish.

In the dream, everyone came to realize that my grandfather was dead. We prepared to carry out his dying wish, which he had written on a large piece of paper on the floor. It said, *"I want you to burn this house down with me in it."* I woke up just after we had crumpled a bunch of newspapers and phone book pages under the coffee table and sparked up a lighter.

Whenever I wake up in the night, I look in Tennessee's direction and find the lump of her tiny body among the blankets and stuffed animals. I reach my hand for her head and leave it there for a moment before moving down to her rib cage. In the otherwise still darkness I wait for her breathing to move my hand up and down a few times. This touch is a reassurance before I go back to sleep, a little ritual to make sure that she is there and alive and safe. It is also another way of connecting to ground.

I want her to know, almost unconsciously, that if she has the same problems that I have that I won't leave her to figure them out on her own. My hand will be there for her, helping her press back against the weight, if or when her eyes are closed tight against the murk that comes down like cold rain. She will come to understand that there is nothing more sinister or beautiful than genetic inheritance. It is natural and robust but also callous and unsympathetic. Because of that, the same disease that has a hold of me may possibly exist within her.

She will want answers to why she feels this way or that way, why she can't seem to shake sadness on otherwise warm and sunny days. Just as I did, she will want to know what the problem is, if it is natural or if things will ever be different. She will want to know if she can fight through it like a tiger at its throat, or if it is best to just wait it out, deal with it as best she can at that moment and not delay in seeking treatment.

I'll tell her, *"Tennessee, I am sorry about this weight, but I wanted so badly for you to be here."*

* * * * *

Epilogue

One cool summer evening I mow the lawn while Tennessee stands framed within the screen of the front door, looking out and waving to me each time I pass. I can see her lips moving: "papa, papa". The sun falls lower as the smell of grass and gasoline spreads like ivy.

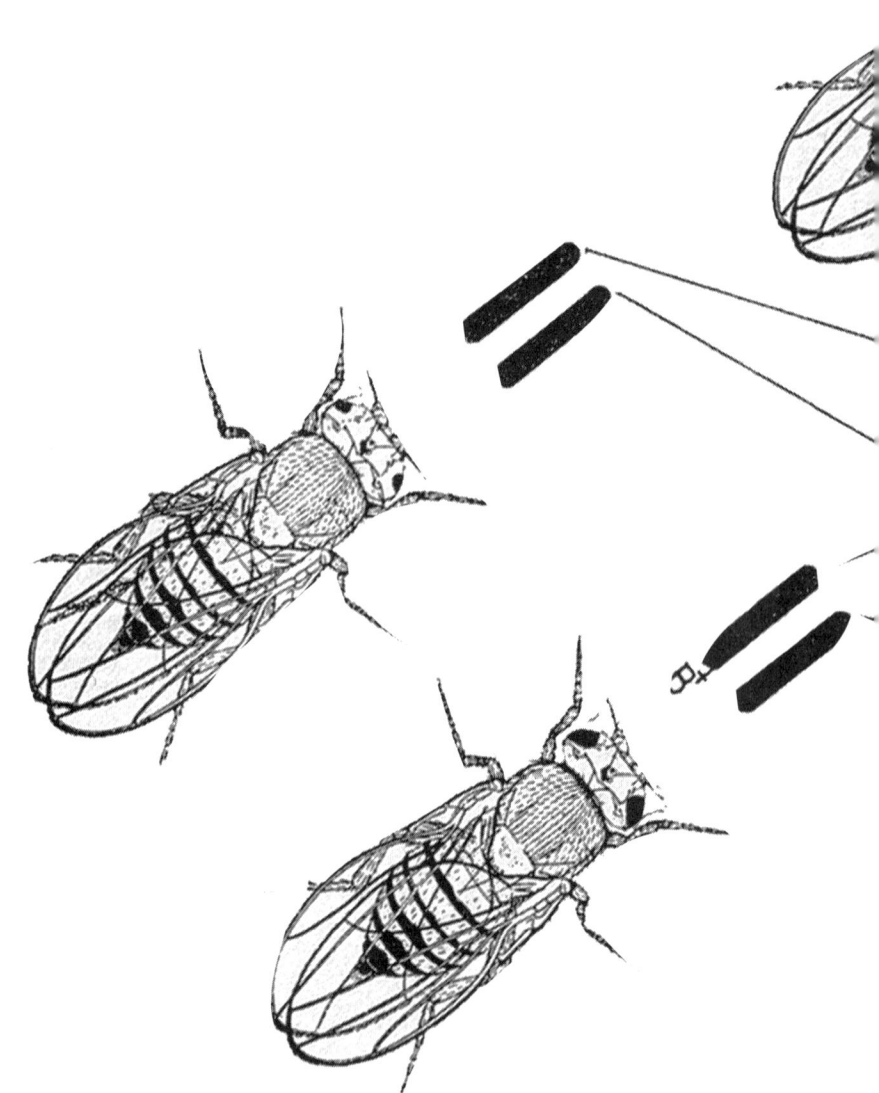

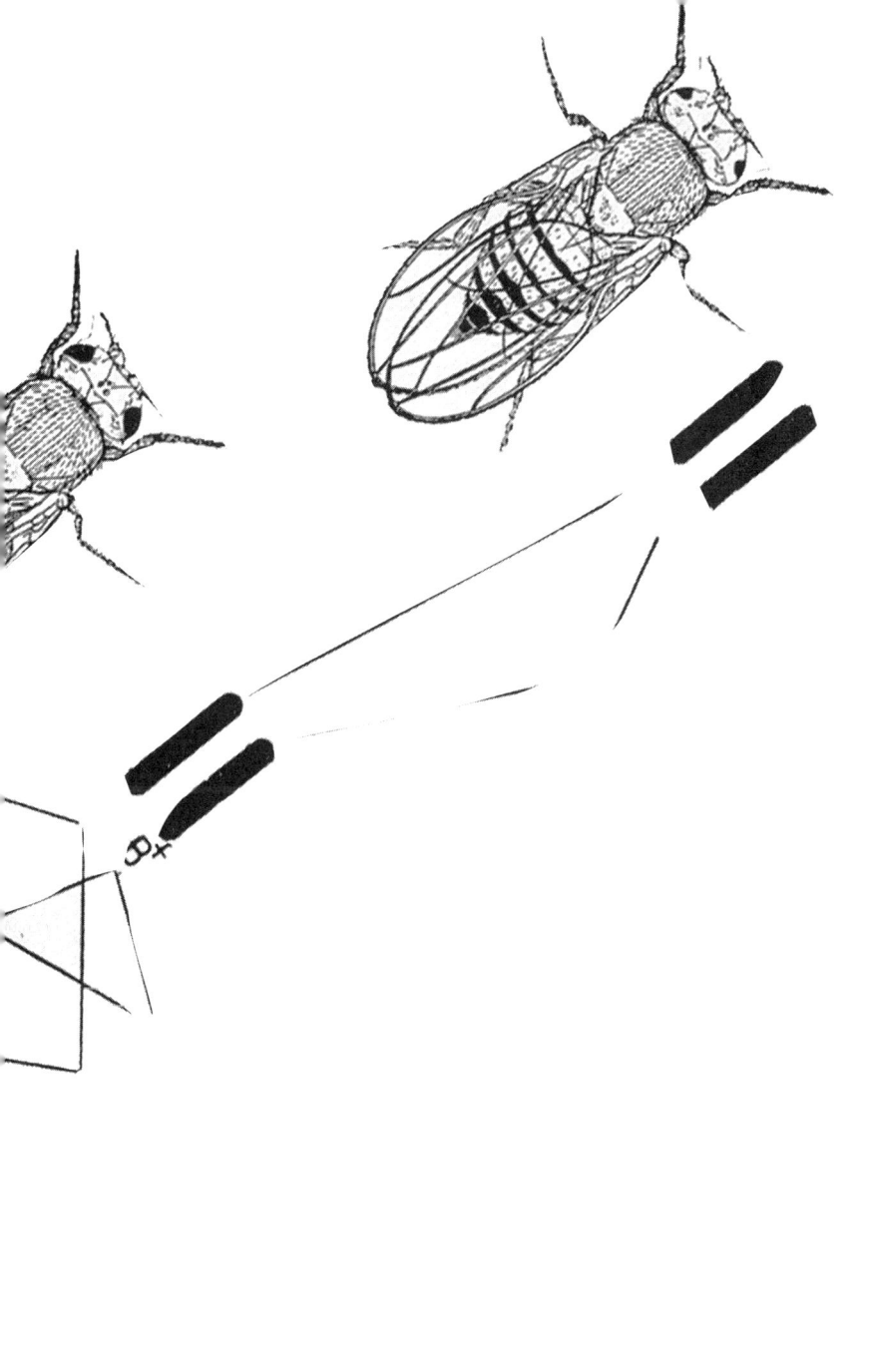

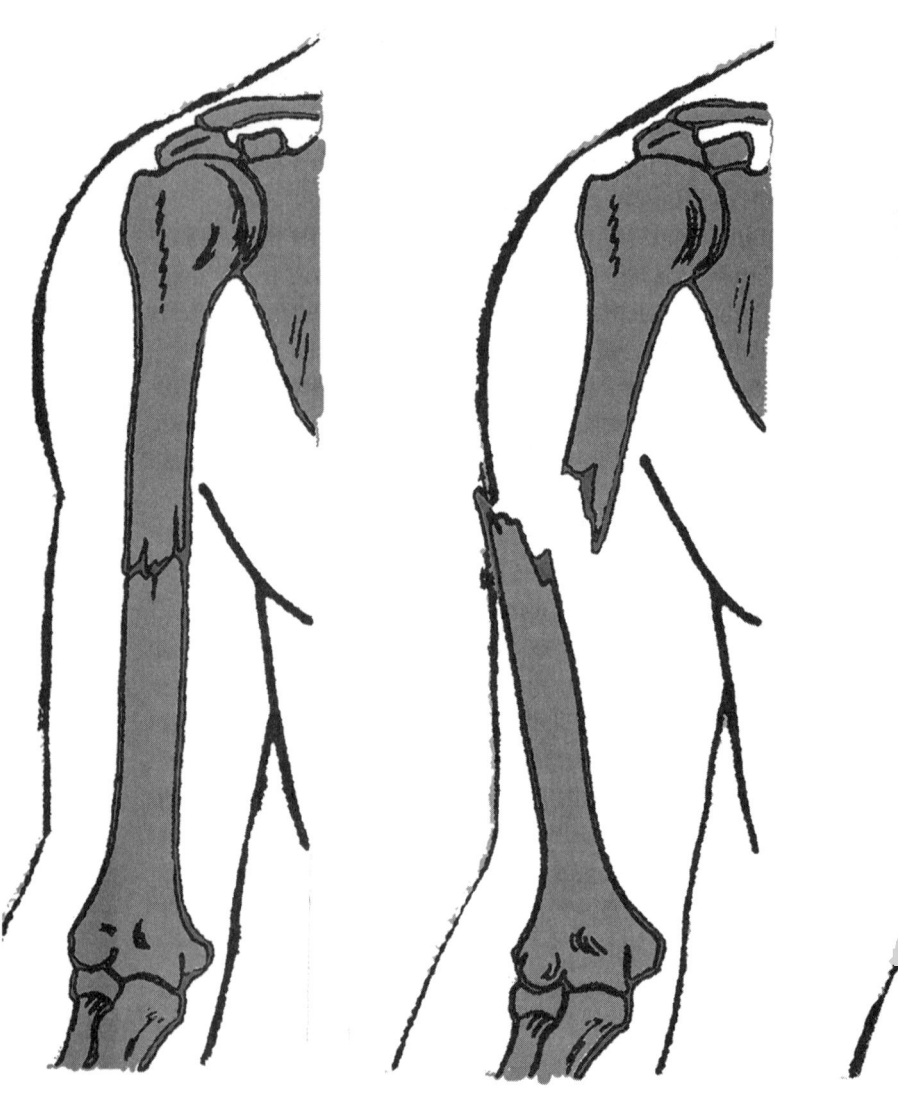

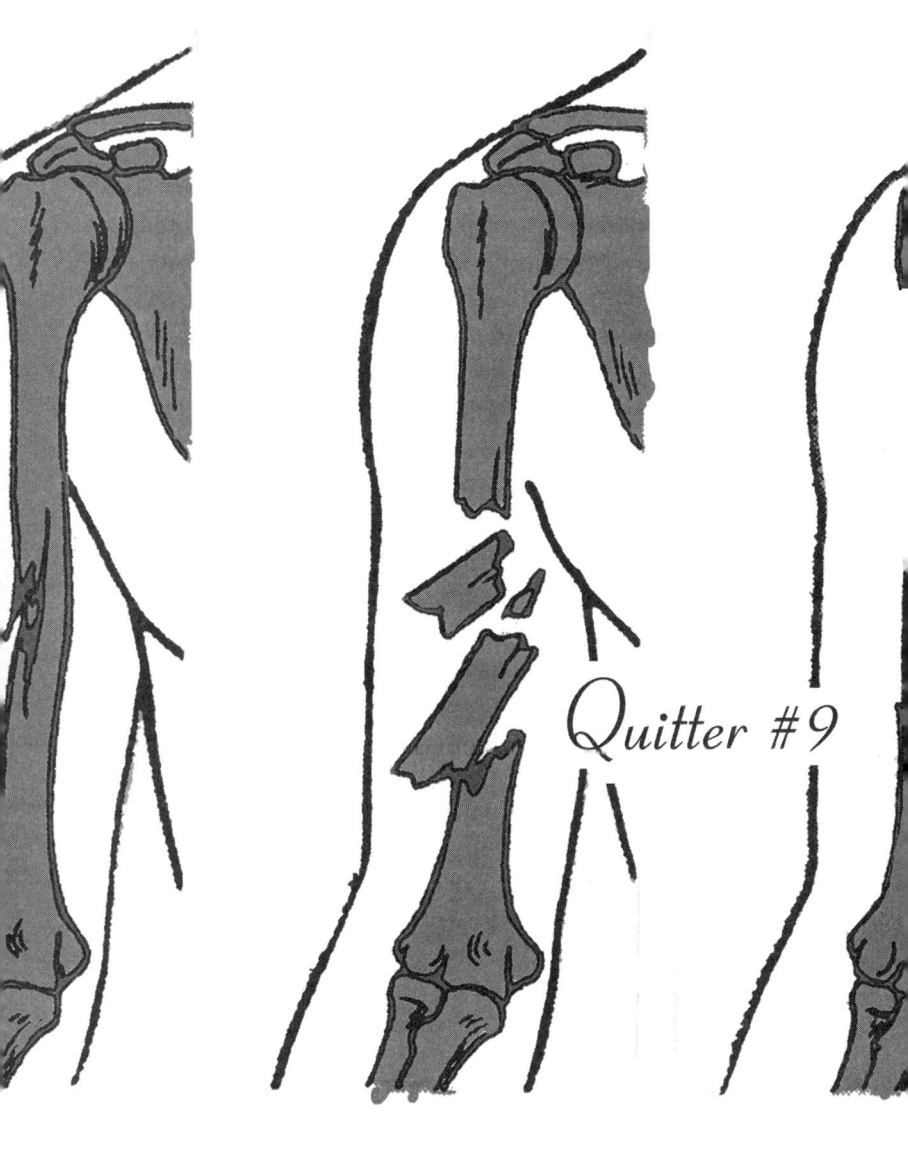

Quitter #9

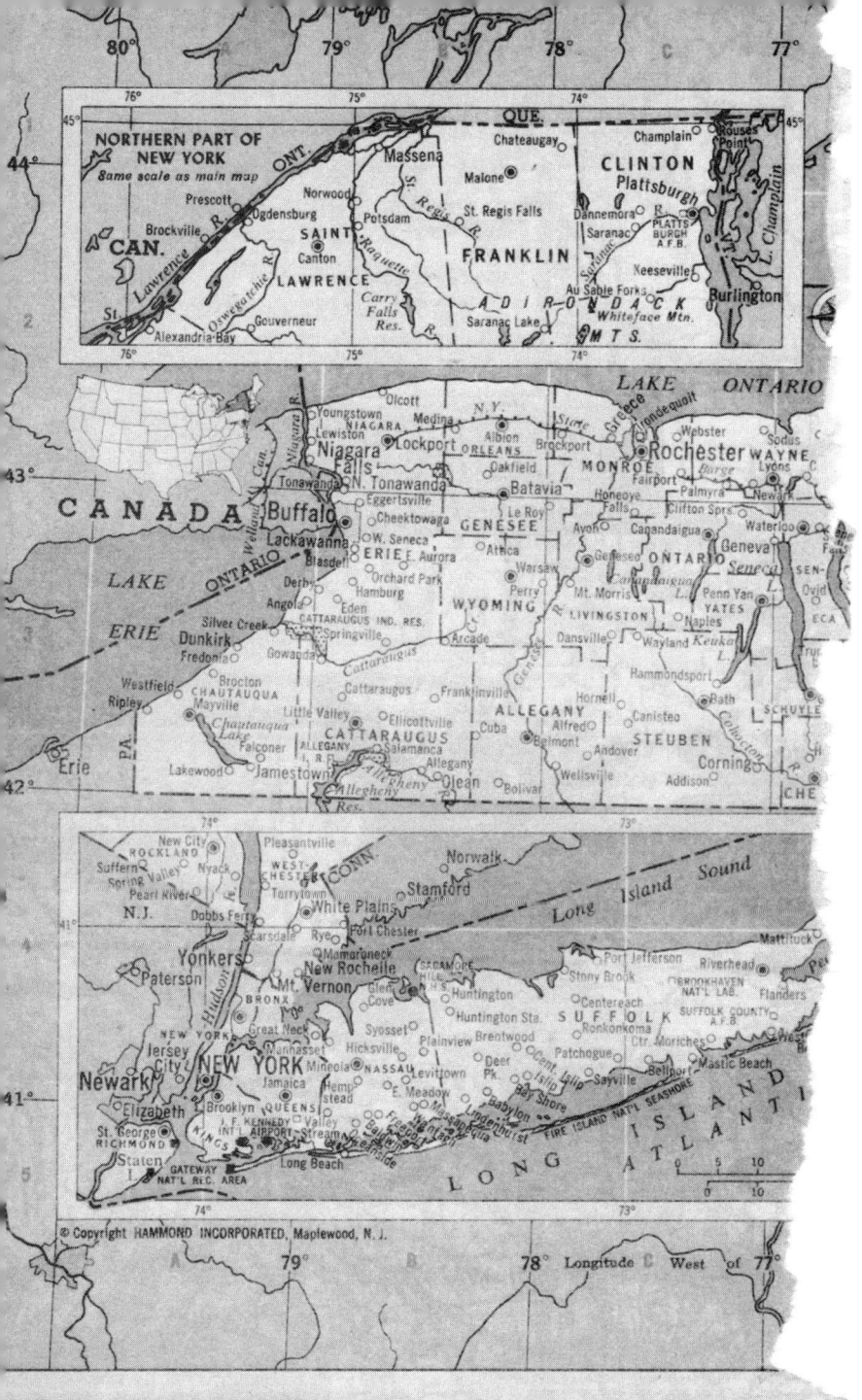

Part One

Winter finally lost its hold on the pasture. The melted snow revealed brown and brittle remnants of milk weed and bull thistle, six months ago strong and thick and rampant, now just dull footnotes of an old season. We step through the weeds without the intent of damage, but our young hearts don't know the thin line we walk between destruction and creation. Stalks shatter loudly under the heels of our small boots. We step into the tree line.

The forest is just starting to grumble back to life and unpack the potential of the coming months. My brother is walking ahead of me. With the gloved heel of his hand he bangs on the thin trunks of moosewood trees that grow up from the soil where the canopy is light. Facing away from me, I can barely hear him talking. I cannot catch his words over the crunch of twigs underneath both pairs of our boots. I imagine him saying we will climb these trees, memorize this forest for a decade to come until beer and cigarettes and drugs steal our interest and lead us out into barren surroundings. But that isn't what he is saying. We keep walking until we reach the edge of the swamp.

Metallic gurgling calls of *konk-la-ree* repeat every few seconds from all through the small wetland. During the fall and winter migrations that minimized the presence of birds, the red wing blackbirds never left. They call this place home all year round. My brother and I get the forest every other weekend, a concession of visitation because of divorce. The easy to spot blackbirds perch sideways on long and flexible cattail stalks. As the birds practice their lines from the old script, I study the soil crumbling from a recently uprooted red maple at the swamp edge and poke at the brown nubs of the dormant cinnamon ferns that bulge from the ground. There is quiet growth here underfoot, cells shaking off the damage of cold and hibernation.

We come to the wet edge; we can now see a quarter mile through to the other side of the swamp. On the south side, a hill climbs up to a lightly wooded plateau where we once found an old bottle dump. We searched it for the cobalt blue medicine bottles that our mother liked to collect but found nothing but a few rusty truck springs and dozens of smashed canning jars. To the west, the forest starts again, dark and full even in the leafless winter. To the east and north are several ways home, all of them as long or short as our patience or hunger makes them.

In the middle of the swamp I watch the chickadees and nuthatches darting among the snags like small thrown stones. The snags are home to woodpeckers and owls during the long days of spring and summer. Now they are quiet. The eerie gray spears hold up the dull, moist sky above us. I look for the sun but can't pinpoint it, its location just a suggestion. With the snow melted, its light just gets sucked into the water like a broken ship.

We stop walking to yell into the swamp and perform with our echoes. We yell things like ***"hey you"*** and ***"shit"*** and *"goddammit"*. We don't yell *"fire"* anymore, not since we stood by the garage and screamed it in unison to amplify the effect. Our father sprinted from the barn and grabbed our shoulders and scanned the area.

"Where? Where is the fire?" We told him there wasn't a fire. He didn't get angry like the time I took my pocket knife to the Paper Birch tree in the side yard and he had to paint the normally white trunk with latex primer to hide the destruction from my step-mother. Or the time my brother used up all the chalk line powder to color his snow fort red. This time he calmed and gathered his breathing. He looked us both intently in the face and explained why you can never yell fire when there is no fire. We nodded. We don't yell fire anymore, anywhere even though when we yell into the swamp no one comes running, nothing we say has importance beyond its boundaries.

We follow the brown edge of the water until we find an isthmus that stabs into the swamp's skin, our boots making a slurping noise each time we raise them from the dark liquid. We breathe heavy with the exertion this part of the walk requires. We enter the meat of the swamp, moving from peninsula to island, from island to rotting log without agenda or goal. We stop occasionally to listen for the snorts of spooked white tailed deer and poke our walking sticks into the mud to test the depth.

I look around and imagine what a few months of longer days can bring. Summer will always be my favorite time to walk the swamps. It smells of both decay and birth and is bursting with both. Turkey vultures circle above us, simple kites tethered to death. Skunk cabbage as tall as my waist grows heavy near the treed edge; warblers, vireos and ovenbirds are thick and busy; the cattails' flower spikes plump with assurance. We pull the flower heads from their leafy sheaths and bang them on tree limbs or each other until they pop, the fluff getting caught up in our hair, our giggling mouths. But now in the heavy gray of winter it seems like the air will always be cold, always make our hands pink and rough like cow's tongues.

* * * * *

When I was very young, the pasture held a horse. My mother wanted the horse even though the family could barely afford it. But they bought it, set up a deal wherein it would be delivered by some old man up the road. My father built a small barn of chipboard and tin, painted it dark red with white trim around the windows. He set the fence posts, ran the light gauge electric wire in an effort to contain the horse on the back edges of the land.

When he poured the barn floor, he had my brother and I set our bare feet next to one another in the wet ce-

ment, permanent reminders that we were once very small. He also drew a heart with his finger and wrote his and my mother's initials along with the year they were married, *"RR + BR 1969"* In 1979, he smashed the initials to dust with a sledgehammer.

During a visit to my house last year, my father, unprompted, told me about the horse. I can only remember it from a few photographs and from the stiff bristled horse brush that remained in the barn long after the horse was gone. The horse's name was Sailor. She was light brown with some white patches. According to his story, my mother only rode the horse a few times, losing interest in it since it wasn't trained. He said he was the one who ended up training the horse, getting it used to having a rider, taking care of its feeding and shelter. He recalls that the horse was gentle; he said he loved her. There was a pause as he thought about it all – the horse, the pasture, the dissolved relationships of the past.

"Your mother secretly quit paying the bills." He looked into his glass of water and saw something I couldn't. *"When the insurance company called and I picked up the phone, they told me the plan had been cancelled. When I found out about the insurance, that's when I found out about everything else."*

He sold the horse shortly after. There was no money for hay and feed. There was no money for much of anything really. He would be divorced and bankrupt not long after the horse was gone. And that was it; this reach back into memory was over. He gave me a much too brief glimpse into an important time in our mutual history, a time that I have no good memories of. I don't know if there was more he wanted to say at that moment. I didn't have any questions ready, any prompts, and we were interrupted. My only child

Tennessee—his fourth grandchild—had awoken from her nap in the other room and sought out his lap. During the fading light of a winter afternoon, we sat across from each other at my dining room table. He held her and called her name, made her giggle there on his knee. When I caught his eye, I knew that my father was trying to tell me something that had nothing to do with a horse.

* * * * *

Over several years, the pasture behind the barn became ungrazed and over grown. The plants that took over in summer were tall and diverse, a chest high jungle during the peaks of rain and heat. From a distance the pasture was homogenous, green. On a windy day the tops of the plants moved like ocean waves, rising and falling towards the pauses of still air. When you came closer, the diversity began to present itself. Oldfield asters and wild bean and goatsbeard formed the edges of the mazes we cut through to the forest to avoid the nettle and burdock.

The steel wire and ceramic insulators that once pretended to hold back the forest are gone, the fence posts removed decades ago and burned. When we are not looking, we still find the white insulators along the old edges of the horse's space. The insulators are rarely intact and generally buried, just an edge of the porcelain sticking up from the soil like a tiny logging whale. Each piece we find acts as a bookmark for some specific chapter in our shared history with the pasture.

"*Remember that time*" – I ask my mother through a Facebook message – "*when JJ and I poked a stick into a hole in the ground behind the barn and it turned out to be a yellow jacket nest? What did we have to get bathed in?*"

Her straightforward answer came later that night. *"A solution of vinegar and meat tenderizer applied to your skin and a warm bath afterwards to bring the stingers out."* She then asked *"why?"* I didn't have a good answer. All I could think was this random fact: I went thirty five years between yellow jacket stings.

* * * * *

Our bedroom in the mobile home was shaped like a horseshoe. The room was divided in half by a closet that held the furnace and the hot water heater. Our beds were arranged on each side of the closet. On one side of the furnace closet sat the toy chest, a small dresser and a lamp. On the other side the long hallway that ran the length of the trailer between the living room and the master bedroom. Our room had two thin pocket doors, each of them sliding noisily in and out of the wall that held them. There were no door knobs, just small circles where you would insert your finger and pull.

One night that I clearly remember, a jar on the dresser containing a half dozen or so fireflies went dark, the sides of the container wet and fogged with respiration. We had forgotten about the insects, left them to die one by one, no more significant to us than a pulled weed in the garden. Their deaths didn't match all the effort we spent seeking them out in the buzzing summer night, laughing and running with our jars held in front of us like stumpy dull swords.

We did not know our own intentions yet, how much power humans hold even at a young age. We were responsible for death, creators of decay in an unnecessary circumstance. Yet there were no philosophers or biologists that night, no one asking *"Did you know that we share cellular devices with plants, with other animals, with the vast domain of insects? That a mitochondrion in one of our brain cells is only slightly different from a mitochondrion in a sugar maple? How is it that you children think you are the only explorers of free will?"* No emancipators came to say, *"Let the fireflies go."*

* * * * *

Above the door knob on the inside of the front door of the trailer, there was an imprint of my father's knuckles. He had punched the door in absolute frustration, slamming the door behind him, throwing bags of his belongings into the back of his orange Ford Pinto. I can't imagine how much that hurt or how upset you have to be to forever stamp the mark of a fist into wood. I couldn't ask him, didn't even know what to ask him. I was five. He was gone.

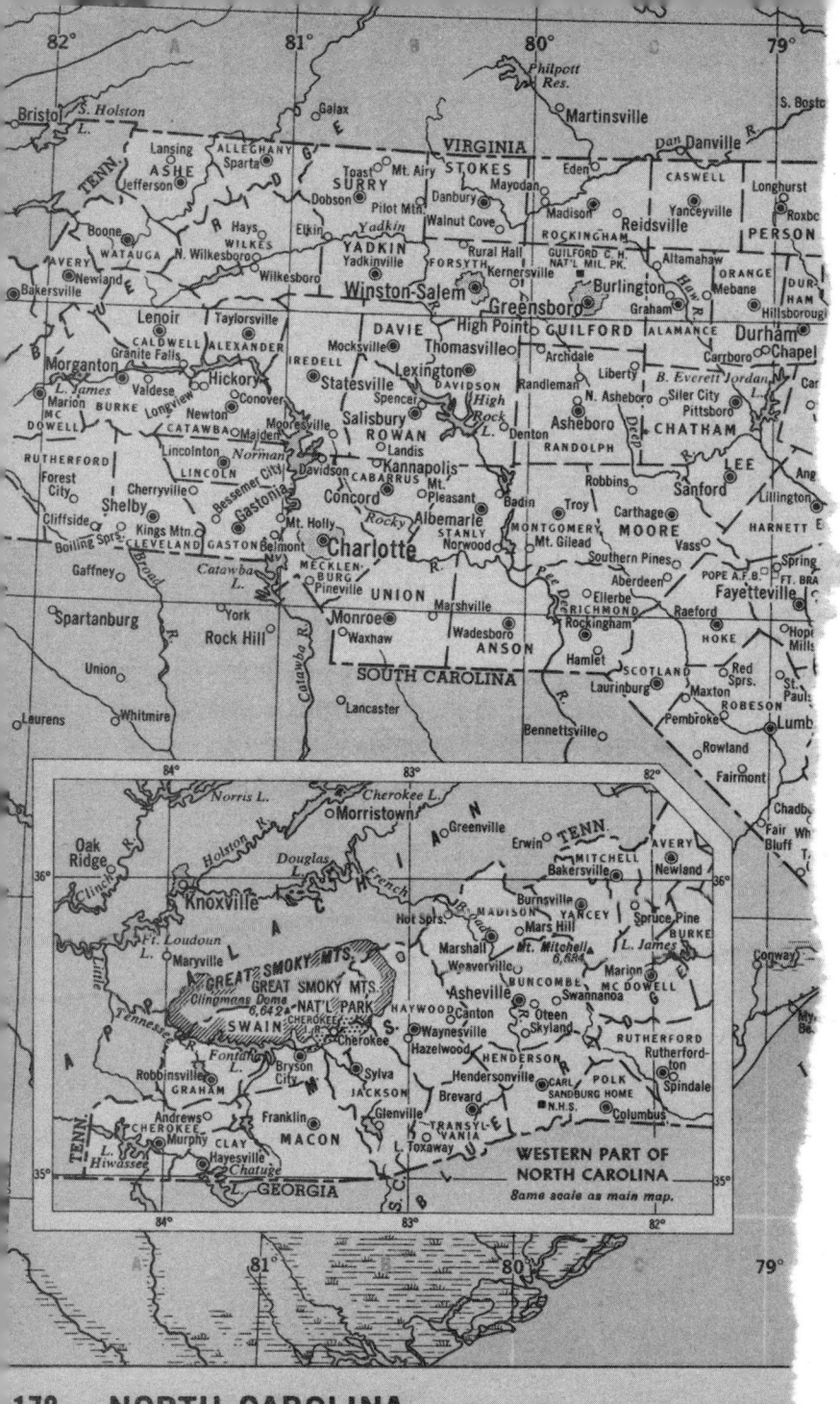

Part Two

Perched upon barn roofs, the black vultures looked like preachers

imperious in a pulpit, wings outspread, the morning dew on their feathers now drying below the sun. The birds were patient, silent; several hundred feet away a road-kill deer awaited their company. I was also there, just as patient, thinking hard about butchering this deer and taking it home to eat.

Pieces of a smashed plastic vehicle grill edged the blacktop of the road. Glass sparkled quietly where the gravel merged with the grass, the edges fluid and undulating like the membrane of a massive amoeba. There were no skid marks on the pavement, no long ruts into the soft weedy shoulder. The driver was long gone, leaving only hints of their movement and direction.

After I spotted the deer and pulled over, I sat in my little white truck for a bit deciding if I would get out and go through with it. I listened to the radio for a few minutes, thinking, sighing, mumbling. I stepped out of the truck, unfolded my pocket knife and locked the blade in place.

The dull brown and white animal lay crumpled in the roadside ditch, its belly bloated by a sunbaked and fermenting stomach. The back legs were broken but splayed out and straight with rigor mortis. The deer looked fake, almost like a discarded lawn ornament. The trash around the deer was ubiquitous—beer bottles, branded fast food containers, various pieces of metal. Old survey flagging hung in the brambles while the tiny remnants of plastic grocery bags chewed up by the county mowers formed a sort of mulch along the ground.

I stood silent and respectful over the dead animal. This was my first attempt at scavenging meat. I thought that maybe I could do it by myself, could figure out all the steps I would need to perform and pull order from an uneasy situation. There was no one around to help me, to talk me through it, to guide my motions. I had recently moved to Siler City, North Carolina, temporarily alone, occupying one room in the decaying remains of an old farmhouse.

I was desperate to exploit my solitude before my partner Kristin and the other landowners joined me a few months later. This deer and its meat and this harvest would be an expression of this time alone, an introduction to a new life and lifestyle. On my own I could easily feed myself with dumpstered food and road kill. I could do it. And if I didn't do it, no one would ever have to know, I would never have to acknowledge to anyone that at one time in my life I pulled my vehicle over, got out and cut open a run over animal on purpose.

My hands shook as I made an incision. I will always remember the butchering skills I learned as a kid, but this was fundamentally different: instead of a clean gunshot or arrow entry, this deer had been hit by a vehicle traveling along at the speed limit or just above, the twists of the road unable to handle speeds faster than that. The impact on the animal had shattered its bones, sending tiny fragments into the flesh. The marrow wept and lungs collapsed, organ utility ceased and whole systems shut down like a rolling blackout. The body cavity filled with blood and bruises formed on the muscles just under the hair and skin. I wasn't thinking about that. I started the process just as I would have with a hunted deer.

Starting with a cut below the anus, I sliced up towards the broken rib cage. Immediately I knew I was going about it wrong. The organs had shifted. By mistake I opened up the stomach. Acorn pieces and bits of bark steamed through the slit and onto my hands. I could almost see the moist stink of rot infiltrate the meat and the hair of the deer, see my time wasted. The meat slowly became ruined and inedible as I moved up and down the body searching to salvage just one piece for the night, just one tiny scrap to make the whole stop worthwhile. It took too long; I continually brought the pit of my elbow up to my nose to combat the smell. I managed to salvage one shoulder piece, resting the small pink and brown slab on the passenger seat of the truck.

When I got home I didn't even eat it.

I know that venison can be prepared in any number of ways—stewed with potatoes and root crops, baked in creamy sauces, pounded out thin with a hammer and lightly grilled over a fire. Here is what I also know: baskets made from tulip popular bark are sturdy and beautiful but ultimately unnecessary outside of devotional primitivism; making cordage from dogbane is meditative but time consuming; drowned opossum is the best type of opossum to eat and it is readily available from farms who use live traps and ponds to protect their chicken flocks; the more you dumpster dive the more you get caught; pigs are amazing, sturdy and friendly creatures that have the potential to escape any containment in order to find you and steal your breakfast; trusting anyone without a bank account or anyone who appropriates crow feathers into their pale, cul-de-sac visages is risky and unadvisable. I learned all this in the three years of my stay at Circle Acres, a rural living collective that failed me, which I both named and put down most of the money to buy. We called it *"the land"*.

* * * * *

I moved to the land first and was alone for two months out there, living a simple and quiet existence. There was no electricity in the room or anywhere on the property. The power pole that was attached to the house had pulled away because of rot around the screws that connected the conduit to the wood. The county electrical inspector told us that they couldn't approve getting the power turned on until it was fixed. Since that part of the house was falling into itself, the idea of repairing it just to plug in a radio seemed pointless. I kept a tiny portable radio in my truck. That served to keep the quiet just out of reach on any particularly lonely time.

I used one cook pot, one plate, one cup, one set of eating utensils. I cooked on either the camp-stove or a small fire and only cooked as much as I could eat in one sitting. To clean myself I would heat water and dump it into a bucket for a sponge bath. I stood naked on the stoop of the house that overlooked the front acre and the road, quickly washing myself as the water cooled. There was quite a bit of freedom in that scene. I never took it for granted. I enjoyed that time alone as much as I could.

The days became shorter. Out there, the darkness of night hung over the land like shade cloth. The light pollution from the Walmart in Siler City looked like a faint orange fog off to the south of the land. That was the only light at night. No street lights, no safety light, just the sun's reflection off the moon or the headlights of a vehicle coming down the gravel road towards the house.

The front acre of our land ran long and thin between the gravel road and a neighbor's wooded land. Before we bought it, someone kept that acre trimmed at a manageable height. Now that we owned it everything out there explored its proper growth potential. Knee high cedar trees stood out green against the dead reeds of summer's grasses.

* * * * *

"I'm not a fucking pioneer," Kristin would say occasionally. *"I can't drain my suburban blood overnight."* Kristin had never lived in the country, never thought she would. She grew up in one of those spokes in the expanding wheel of suburbia that currently positions New Hanover County, North Carolina on the list of top five worst metro areas in the nation for sprawl. When it looked like buying land would be an actuality, the possibility just waiting for pen to hit paper and money to transfer, I brought her in close for a serious questioning.

"Are you sure you will be okay out in the country? Is this really what you want? It can get very... lonely."

"We can't be lonely together, can we?"

The first time I ever saw Kristin she was making fancy drinks at a coffee shop in downtown Wilmington. I walked there every Saturday and Sunday morning, creaking out of my apartment, a plastic mug in hand, quiet and silently sick of being alone when I woke up.

Under her breath she commented on the black and white sticker on my mug: *"Capitalism Kills Me."* I didn't hear what she said exactly, but years later she recalled that she thought I was a poser, a souvenir hunter in the gift-shop of anarchism. She says she didn't think much of me. I didn't think of her much either, really. Too young for me, just another college kid with an attitude and a problem with everything. She poured my coffee once or twice a week, and I walked out the world no different than before, the two of us just a set of barely connected lines amongst thousands of others, seemingly random squiggles that turn out to be the strongest knots.

We officially met years later at a weekend activist retreat held in a small cottage on the Intercoastal Waterway. To contribute to the meals, I brought a small bag of hand-picked but dumpstered bagels. She brought an entire trash bag of bagels from the same source. She saw me smirk and shake my head, a sign that her move of dumping thirty pounds of bagels onto the kitchen counter was commendable.

We talked all that night, sitting on a boat dock, our feet draped over the rough wooden the edges, mine moving nervously over the dark and silent water. A voice came from a bench behind us.

"I didn't know it was possible to have so many stories about dumpster diving."

At the end of the retreat, Kristin handed me a scrap of paper with her telephone number on it. Underneath the number she wrote *"call me or I'll think you're an asshole."* This time I smiled and my stomach growled as adrenaline shot through me. She ended up calling me first, just a few days later. I invited her over, but I wasn't ready for her visit. She used the bathroom, came out and remarked *"nice underwear"*. I had left a pile of clothes on the bathroom floor and hadn't thought to pick it all up before she came over. After that we were inseparable.

We spent a lot of time sitting on the roof of abandoned condominiums abutting the Cape Fear River. The sound of vehicles crossing the Cape Fear Memorial Bridge roared off to the south of us. Back to back we leaned on each other atop the shingled peak of the roof. *"What do you think of when you look out?"* Her voice was near my ear. When our heads touched I could feel the slight vibration of the words as they left her mouth, a hum like a mass of bees swarming. The warmth and sweat of her back was right against mine. I could smell her unadorned body odor; she smelled like crayons. Sometimes she still does. That is how I know she is nervous. The crayon smell comes out strong and stands there on its own, triggering me to come close, and to hold tight.

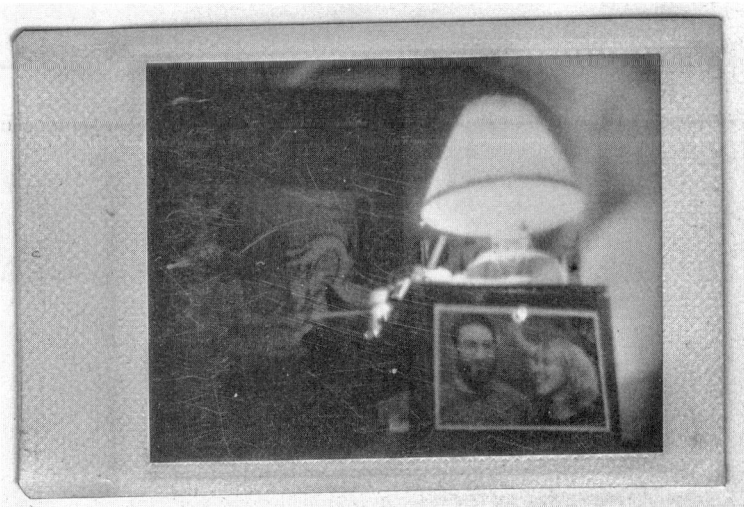

FOG INDEX

TRACE RAMSEY

#1

Sunday morning

With bumblebees, all but the queens die before winter. They emerge from their underground burrows and immediately begin to feed on the pollen and nectar of the early perennial flowers that rise along with them. Purple deadnettle and bluebells are some of the first to appear in the memory of the last frost; their colors are prominent in the otherwise brown and drab setting. In our front yard, the bumblebees hover close to the flowers, then land and begin the work that they have never not known: feed, find a home, lay eggs, rule.

Tennessee and I watch closely as the bees poke their faces into the organs of the flowers. The bees rise from their meals and buzz near our faces, hovering close by, wondering about our intentions. We are not like the other bees. Tennessee thinks they are sniffing us and asking us to play. She giggles that toddler giggle that means you don't have to understand any of this in order to enjoy it. Sometimes it is better to be ignorant, trustful, and welcoming instead of knowledgeable and destructive. These queens mean us no harm; outside of that, may all the queens drown.

Tennessee and I leave the bees and go in search of redbuds along the creek behind the house. I lift her as high as I can above my shoulders so that she can pick and eat the sweet red flowers. She quickly eats the lower buds and asks me to hold her higher. I do my best. She practices her take on slash and burn, grazing the reachable edibles until there is nothing left. She has exhausted everything that the two of us combined are able to grab. But Ten wants more. She cries when I set her down. I point up at the empty branches, open my hand and show her the definition of empty. I try to explain the concept of finite. At two years old she just doesn't care. She shuffles through the grass in search of violets and dandelions.

Yellow pine pollen drifts along every surface and crease. It sticks in the grooves of car windows and headlights, covers the porch steps like spilled flour. The grass blades of the yard where we walk have yellow outlines, highlights of days and nights of tree and shrub intercourse. Green inchworms hang from every tree limb and power line, their little green bodies floating down in search of meals but finding only our face as we walk. Tennessee pauses as each worm lands on her clothing. She coaxes the creatures onto her fingers and the backs of her hands. Ten stands tall, holding the tiny strings of the worms, wiggling the puppets of the short wind of spring.

Tobacco, NC, and 2015

From an open window I watch as two robins move their fight from the street and into the front yard of my house. They are males establishing territory and permissions to nest within sight of the other. They are surprisingly quiet. Their actions are full of sharp action, deliberate glides, open beaks. The bands around their eyes are bright white and thin. Their orange chests are dark, almost red, puffed up and out in a visual display that is easy to understand and anthropomorphize.

An old man walks the sidewalk, smoking a long, recently lit cigarette. He scares off the birds as he enters the scene from my right. The robins disappear up and out of view, most likely into a nearby sweet gum tree. Through the open window I can smell the man's smoke even as he leaves my view. The way the smell travels is indistinct, the physics of it beyond my knowledge. All I know is that the odor reminds me of dozens of places and people and times, not only here in North Carolina, but of New York dive bars and mountain cabins and old trucks travelling slow into the city. It reminds me of my father when he was thin and my brother when he was using. It reminds me that I will never remember what I was thinking every time I decided to get pass-out drunk.

The Blue Flower

Tennessee runs to me, her outstretched fist holding several stems of musk hyacinth. *"Can we eat this, Papa?"* She learns the flowers in the yard by asking over and over if she can eat this one or that one. I tell her that it isn't the flower that is edible on this particular plant. She drops the fragrant little bluebells at my feet and pulls purple dead-nettle from its vined mat near the driveway. She snaps the flowers right into her mouth without looking at me. This motion is directly attributed to her latest knowledge, that the purple dead-nettle is edible. She also knows that the square stem puts this plant in the mint family and that a person can eat just about everything with that telltale square stem. Tennessee moves on to a patch of violets that were somehow missed during the last pass and from there to a dull yellow dandelion bud that only wants to go to seed.

Living With Your Father

I learned to parallel park in the same driveway that I learned to ride a bicycle. My father removed the training wheels unceremoniously and never reattached them. He held me on the bike as I came down the slight incline of the driveway and towards the unfinished garage. He let go. I pedaled. He stood there in the driveway. I made it beyond the garage and into the grass. Even when I eventually fell by the willow tree I knew that I had been freed of something.

*****

In the fall of 1996 my father and step mother gave me a car. It was their 1985 Oldsmobile Calais sedan. It was blue. My brother had crashed my first car into ditch after a night of putting substances into his body that he will still not admit to. *"I fell asleep"* is what he usually says. *"I fell asleep at the wheel."* I bought that car when I was sixteen with the entirety of my life savings at that point— $1,600. Four years later that car went to the scrap yard. I bought my next car for $150. It lasted for about as long as you can expect a $150 car to last. Even though it was mostly not running, I sold it for $200 to a crew of migrant farm workers. They got it up and going. My father said he saw that car everywhere for years and years later.

So the Calais was just sitting there, a balding reminder of my childhood. My father didn't want anything for it. I think he knew it didn't have much left to give even though I certainly had a lot to ask of it. Most of the paint on the hood had peeled up in large and small pieces, the stripes merging and fading and merging again like some blue and gray metal zebra. Rust holes rounded and divoted like golf balls hid underneath the frame. Rust ate the bottom edges of all the doors, the trunk rim and the bumpers. The radiator was held in place by stubborn habit alone, and pieces of rust the size of pennies swam in the coolant stream. The doors didn't lock and the horn didn't work. It wouldn't start if it was too hot or too cold. Without thinking about all that, I loaded it with all of my belongings and my fiancé and a promise of a new era and drove 734 miles south.

Goodbye

Thousands of red clover mites crawl around on the warm concrete stoop of our front porch. The mites are tiny but easy to see and watch because they are so red. Their entire bodies are red; pressing down on them to crush them with a forefinger leaves a red stained streak along the somewhat smooth surface of the painted concrete. I smash and drag, smash and drag, smash and drag individual mites, caught up in this simplistic ritual of killing the insignificant.

Tennessee comes out the front door and sits down next to me on the brick steps. She asks what I am doing; I come out of this trance of murder. I tell her she can't smash them like I do. I think about that, how now I seem able to judge that she is suddenly not allowed to commit to her basest human instincts. I talk her out of squashing the mites by telling her that they are related to ticks and spiders, that they are not insects but in the category and classification of true mites. Telling her how things live and work usually helps to transition us away from difficult subjects.

"They can't bite you or hurt you, sweet one. I can't really tell you why I was killing them. I mean, I could tell you but it won't really make any sense."

"What will happen to them now, Papa? Now that they are dead?"

The Pit

1.

It is that time of winter when I miss spider webs and those big roaches that pop when you step on them on the sidewalk. This is the worst part of winter, the time when you know that it is the worst part and it is happening right now. This is the coldest it will be, the cloudiest, the most threatening of snow and freezing rain. It is also the time when most of the day is in darkness. I sit on the couch and watch the birds drain the feeders that hang from the overhang of the front porch. The birds are cold and hungry and drawn to those cylinders full of seeds and dried fruit pieces. My child Tennessee is at the window repeating the names of the birds as I identify them. She already knows many of them by sight.

"Who is that, Ten?"
"House sparrow."
"And that big one that is making a mess?"
"Red bellied woodpecker."

In the gray there is still color; in the leafless trees there is growth waiting. In me there is a fight to reach out beyond myself.

2.

The garden is rooting and sprouting. I have just planted the tomato and pepper plants. I interspersed basil seedlings throughout the deep bed. I walk the lengths of the raised beds every day and pull the weeds just when they emerge, when they are tender and weak. I like to keep the garden clean and the competition for water and nutrients skewed toward the food plants. I know that some of the weeds can be eaten as well. Wood sorrel is prevalent, but I can't eat much of it. It is sour and contains a compound that—in large amounts—is not good for a person. Then there is the wiregrass, a weed that is next to impossible to eradicate. Any little piece of the plant, whether it is root or leaf, can and will become a new plant. It spreads rapidly. It digs in. It is a physical metaphor for depression. You just can't ever get completely clear of it. I can keep it managed, plucking the sour moods as they pop up and before they can root and thrive.

3.

The red bellied woodpecker seems to be a slow tapper. I watch it as it methodically digs into the soft wood of our neighbor's dying oak tree. That house has been vacant for over a year now. The only life present is what we can see in the trees and bushes. In the winter, the empty branches of the trees are full of puffed up mourning doves. They brace against the cold wind and rain with no protection other than what they were born with: feathers, follow bones, small and simple brains.

4.

"I already saw the woodpecker hole, Papa."
"You don't want to watch it build the nest? That hole is perfectly round."

"I already saw it, Papa."
"OK, I'll watch is myself then."

I stand at the fence and watch. Behind me, Tennessee moves soil from one end of the garden to the other. I don't stop her. Kristin comes out the back-door and stands on the concrete patio. Her hands are on her hips, supporting her pregnancy. She notes that the mourning doves are making their awful noises. A long time ago she thought they were owls. When I pointed out that they were not, the mourning dove became her least favorite bird, maybe even her least favorite creature of all.

"Even worse than ticks?"

QUITTER/TEN

IAMNOT
ATALKER

AGE/FORTYONE

There is a low fog and the front yard is a mix of glitter and broken glass shining up from the individual blades of grass. The street is quiet. The furnace hums below us as the vents near the floor growl with warm air. My partner Kristin and our daughter Tennessee eat French toast at the dining room table and debate lightheartedly about the taste of the syrup and the shapes of the shards of butter that melt on their plates. Tennessee giggles and talks with her mouth full of bread. Outside, the first fledgling house sparrows are clumsy in the white clover. As their parents fly near with food, the young ones' mouths open just like fish about to come down hard on a lure.

It is spring; the bottoms of our feet are always dirty. We track potting soil and saw dust and mulch through the house, little trails of crumbs to indicate the day's activity.

There is constant squeaking of the screen door hinges. We come in and out; flies and bees take the same route.

Winter is over, that dark time of the year when I miss spider webs and those big roaches that pop when you step on them on the sidewalk. The heat is coming, the heat that makes a person wish it was winter all over again, the occasional desire for little pieces of other seasons to appear whenever we need them to or want them to: an icicle to rub on my forehead when the sun is high and relentless; a wash of humidity when the world is leafless, the sun small and cold.

AGE/THIRTYNINE

A horse chestnut aged slowly in the front yard of my grandparents' house on Maltby Road. With just a bit of pressure, its shabby bark flaked off in palm-sized pieces revealing bright orange below dull gray. The tree matched the asphalt siding of the house, gloomy and coarse. Both tree and house are gone now, taken over by a field in which a farmer rotates crops of corn, soybeans, and wheat. My father says that each fall the bedroom where he grew up now sprouts in rows of corn. I imagine the soil stubbled like a great unshaven face and my father envisioning his bed among the crops.

Several years ago, I looked up the house address to see a current Google street view. On the computer screen appeared a space of field and sky, an unrecognizable place where so many times I ran under that horse chestnut, gathered its seeds and hulls, touched its sticky growing buds in spring. I remembered that in a stiff autumn wind, the horse chestnuts fell like coins from a change purse. My brother, cousins, and I would load the pockets of our sweatshirts with the seeds and chase each other as fast as we could. I would throw the seeds at their backs, listening for the dull *whump* of a connecting hit. They would return throws in my direction. The exchange would end in hard breathing all around. We would stand there bent in half, our hands gripping our knees, each of us panting and laughing into the developing dusk. The next day our shoulders would burn. But that night we would wipe the sweat from our faces and go eat baked beans with bacon and onions on top.

Most of the outer shells of the horse chestnut seeds remained attached to the tree, blackening in that space above us, slowly decaying in the branches. From below, the thousands of open casings look like regurgitating birds feeding their young. Through the years, we boys regarded the rare seed that fell from the tree with the outer hull intact as a special and powerful weapon. We hardly ever threw those at each other. Instead, we kept these special chestnuts on dresser tops or closet shelves until the outer layer turned black and fell away, revealing the glossy dark seeds inside. The seeds themselves eventually desiccated, shriveling from the inside in the absence of the requirements for growth: light, water, desire.

A seed is stored life. One of my farmer friends says a seed is, metaphorically, the promise of a future. In Southern folklore, splitting the seed of a native persimmon straight down the middle reveals a prediction of the type of winter to come. Finding the shape of a spoon tells of a heavy wet snow, the spoon therefore representing a shovel. The shape of a knife indicates icy winds, the knife symbolizing the wind cutting into you. The shape of a fork is the most desirable. The fork tells of a mild winter and the possibility of a small amount of light snow. I can't remember what the fork means to symbolize. It doesn't really matter to me: after splitting dozens of persimmon seeds over several different years, I never found a shape that was anything other than a spoon.

That horse chestnut tree died in an ice storm in 1991, the same year my grandfather died alone in a nursing facility just north of Attica. I was a junior in high school working nights at one of the two grocery stores in town. My boss sent flowers. We boys—brothers and cousins—sat in the back of the funeral home and told each other dirty jokes.

*****

My father and his twin brother made a trek to see the Maltby Road house before the volunteer fire department used it as a practice burn. It had been vacant for years. During their visit, they felt the need to touch the dusty counter tops and peer beyond bedroom doors. They opened closed drawers, checked old newspapers for the date. They touched everything familiar, but they didn't recognize themselves in that space. My father told me that he never felt so distant from himself, so simply removed from his own history even as it physically confronted him.

As kids, we visited the house often. My father's house and the Maltby Road house were in two different towns but connected by one road and one right hand turn. My brother and I sometimes biked the distance. Even with all the visits, the house exists in fragile memory for me. Since I never lived in the house, I borrowed my connection to it in a way, all fun, and no pain. It exists differently for my father, in very distinct ways. When he was five, he suffered through rheumatic fever in his tiny bedroom, which ruined his heart forever. On the front porch, he listened as his twin brother read a draft notice. In the family room he watched daily as his mother sat and drank a gallon of wine, gradually becoming glossy eyed and abusive.

I was nearly the same age as my daughter Tennessee when I last saw my grandmother. She lay flat on a hospital bed parked edge long between the couch and the television in the front room of the house. On the outside of the house, that wall faced the road, the windows catching a marking of sunlight through the empty branches of the horse chestnut tree. I viewed my grandmother's body in curiosity and apathy. She had spoken and carried on loudly in life, the cough of her cigarette ruined lungs rattling throughout the massive house even in her last days. In death, her dormant frame hushed the room. In the silence, I stood looking out the screen door watching the cars and tractors pass by, their transience a convenient assurance of the fundamentals: we are never truly alone and everyone dies.

The brothers left the place as it had existed for years—blank, stale, purged of the warm blood that used to cycle through it. Vines grew through broken windows. The floors had damp spots and stains from countless leaks in the roof. The walls grew wild with a mixture of unfurling wallpaper and black mold. Beetles and crickets multiplied behind the walls. Then the Oakfield volunteer fire department burned it down.

Most of the people who had ever lived in that house were long dead. My father and uncle had moved away healthy and single, ready to live. Now my father's body carries a pacemaker and forty-five years' worth of daily alcohol use; his twin brother—ears ruined in Vietnam, knees crumbling from decades of driving an Agway feed truck—awaits a new kidney. Just like the house, they can't escape age and disrepair for too much longer. As for the others – the parents who raised them, the brothers and sisters who shared the supper tables and the arguments and the four walls of the house – they are buried in Oakfield and Pittsburgh and Rochester and Elba. They were all buried with shovels; the house was buried with a backhoe.

*****

"Do you mind if we take the long way?" I asked, even though Kristin wouldn't know the long way from the short way. We were driving to Buffalo for my sister's wedding rehearsal. There was plenty of time, no reason to rush. I made sure we left early just so I could drive down roads that I had not travelled in a very long time.

"Sure, why?"

"There's something I want to drive by and look at." My father told me what had happened to my grandparents' house on Maltby Road, but I needed to see it for myself. I spent so much time at that house that it was just amazing to me that it could be completely gone. The process of the house disappearing was incredible, burned up so that people could practice what to do when it really mattered, could crawl low through the smoke in full gear and feel that heavy heat.

Kristin never saw the Maltby Road house even though it still stood during the early part of our relationship. We were too wrapped up in learning about our immediate selves and how we fit together to even think about remote family homes located five states away. She never knew the road's name or that it had any importance to me or herself or Tennessee. She hadn't met my father's father and probably couldn't guess his name. But she could easily pick him out from a lineup of old white men. My father shares his father's features—the jawline, the forehead, the ears, the brown eyes. Even with my green eyes, my face is following the same course. The only thing that makes me stand out is my full head of subtly graying hair; both my father and grandfather went bald well before forty.

As we drove, unfamiliar new homes marked the road on each side. My stomach churned. I knew we were close, but the unfamiliar made me question whether we had already passed it by. I only recognized the home's former position after topping an easy-sloped hill with a small bridge at the bottom. Orange and black warning signs on each corner marked the narrowing of the road at the bridge. When I saw it I knew where we were. I found a rough, stony pull-in where the driveway used to be, now a bare patch of ground used as a place to turn tractors around and attach implements. I didn't recognize anything; there was nothing to look at anyway. Years of plowing and disking pulverized any small remains of the charred house.

"This is it?"

"Yeah, this is it."

We don't stay long and don't get out of the car. I try to tell her what it all used to look like, how we all played in the massive yard or slid down the creek bank to hear our echoes under the bridge or catch and release crayfish with little glass jars. But mostly I just think to myself, think how the creek below the bridge is shallow and full of massive flattened rocks that come up out the water. I think about how the tops of the rocks are dry and bright like the exposed skulls of poorly buried giants.

*****

Across from my father's house, three crows fight off a hawk in the remnants of a hedgerow. What used to be several small fields separated by trees, rocks, and brambles is now one consolidated and wind-bothered chunk of land. What were once tractor and foot trails inside the hedgerow are now just other parts of this ground, this monotonous field of whatever.

The hawk holds on to a volume of sky. I see the crows' wings flapping, imagining how the bones click in the sockets, hollow and brittle and built only for flight. Their low scolding caws come through the air to us as we sit on the front porch, the soil below the birds still dark orange and slightly shiny from a recent deep plowing. Kristin asks me what I'm thinking.

"I'm trying to just look and watch and think about nothing, but all I can think of are the names of all the birds in the crow family."

She laughs.

Corvidae," I pronounce. *"Crows, jays, ravens and magpies. Scavengers all; obligate opportunists."*

"Bird nerd."

"Did you know that crows' beaks don't work well at puncturing skin?"

"I love you." She looks toward the crows and beyond. It is late May and the grass in the front yard is just starting to green. Leaf buds and Japanese beetles multiply in the trees above. Along the road's edge, milkweed comes up thin and pale green like asparagus. Later that evening we start talking about having another child while Tennessee sleeps between us.

AGE/TEN

I lived part of my childhood in a plain, vinyl-sided double wide at the corner of Griswold and West Bergen Roads in Western New York. From a distance, the black vinyl shutters bordering each window were meant to look like real wood. The house itself floated above an acre of old farmland that my mother and stepfather bought from his brother. Before the house arrived, the land was cleared and dusty.

Ours was one of the first of a quick influx of modular homes into the area. Trailers screaming *"WIDE LOAD"* peppered the back roads of the vast and sparsely populated areas of Genesee, Livingston, and Wyoming counties. The trucks, often traveling in long convoys, filled our country roads with the same shapes, cinder block chimneys, and gravel driveways. Creativity was over.

Despite appearances, I never really thought of it as a real house. At the same time, my father was building a home on Miller Road from the ground up—his own hands laying brick and running wire—under paid workers built this modular home in some out-of-state factory. My mother and stepfather selected a design from a glossy catalog. The cover of a brochure addendum proclaimed *"All You Need Is Land!"* and offered the possibility of easy financing direct from the manufacturer.

The builder held a cash deposit, signed off on a receipt. They all agreed on a delivery date, had a basement excavated, septic lines dug and buried, installed the power pole. We all stood near the road as the house arrived on two separate flatbed trucks, red caution flagging draped over the back ends like garish necklaces. Hazard lights whirled from the cabs as the diesels idled on the soft shoulder of the road. A man with dirty fingernails appeared with a thin stack of paperwork. Someone took a few Polaroid photos.

The installation crane arrived earlier in the day, the operator and crew caffeinated and ready to attach thick steel lines to each corner of what would become the back piece of the house. The crane lifted a long rectangle several yards into the air, slowly moving it into place on top of the damp concrete block walls of the basement. The two halves merged, the siding on each end patched and joined, the installers doing the best they could to make it seamless. Inside, the installers noted and patched all the drywall cracks, laid out the carpet, unboxed and plugged in the appliances. My stepfather signed a few documents and received a small manila envelope containing several copies of the door keys. This thing was now home, all of us looking on as the workers finished bolting it all down to the old hay field.

That field was more slate rock and limestone than soil at that point, the once productive and fertile loam reduced to a rocky desert from years of agricultural abuse. Grass seed refused to take during the first year; a dusty sadness grew instead. The house lounged there, bright white among one full acre of practically nothing, just patchy weeds here and there, and the beginnings of a small sumac hedge on one of the road edges. My stepfather planted two sickly maple trees in the front yard. Despite my brother and me dumping several five-gallon buckets of water on the trees twice a day, the maples never thrived. We ripped them out during the next summer's drought.

Thirty years later, a Google map shows one short, lonely tree in that yard on Griswold Road.

AGE/FORTY

The blood dripping into the toilet changed to bright red from dull brown. Kristin thought she might be miscarrying, and I thought I could have known what that felt like. But I couldn't know. I didn't have the equivalent basis to experience it. I had never lost something that was part of my physical being. What Kristin felt was the biological cleaving of a potential human being, our potential child.

Kristin called the birth center to speak with the midwife.

"I'm eleven weeks pregnant. I think I might be miscarrying. I want to find out what I should do, what my options are." She hung up, said they would call back.

She looked over at me. *"It could be worse. I could be dying."*

You are dying, I thought. I am dying. This new child was either dying or dead already. Kristin arched her back with a strong exhale. *"Ok, it is officially cramps. I can't deny it anymore."*

I knew pure helplessness.

*****

The fetus was the size of a bumblebee, gray and sticky with small black eye dots like poppy seeds. We could see the ribs, the limbs, the skull in early formation. It all happened fast; Kristin's water broke and there it was on her pad. Still in shock, we looked at it and expressed our amazement at its features, its appearance.

The viewing of the fetus in our hands was otherworldly, fake, and absurd. We moved quickly from pure wonder to the recognition of loss. We knew that this child was never coming back; we had to tell Tennessee that this child was never coming back. She understood the concept of yesterday, the concept of loss. For her, time is still something that ravels instead of unravels, an accumulation. Everything, no matter how insignificant, is something to remember.

"Should we bury it?"

"Of course we should bury it."

We grabbed shovels from the shed and walked silently to the front yard.

AGE/NINE

The morning light made the backs of the grackles shine like weak light bulbs below the sweet gum tree. Their greasy calls penetrated the thin windows watching over our front porch. My daughter Tennessee—three years old and as many feet tall—pressed her face against the glass of the window nearest me. She smashed her nose flat and breathed heavily from her mouth, perhaps felt the sensation of cartilage pressing between bone and cold glass. I sat in the rocking chair beside her, the one with the dingy gray pillow made hairy by sleeping cats.

I placed my coffee cup on the windowsill below her face. The steam from the cup brought out nose and handprints from previous mornings spent peering out, watching stray dogs run in the street and birds emptying the feeders hanging from the porch eaves.

It was late autumn in Durham North Carolina. Dark-eyed juncos and white-throated sparrows had returned to the area as they moved slowly south, their northern nests all spent and fallen as the elements returned their building materials back to the ground. The birds spread through the front yard and to the edges of the street. Beyond and above them, the leaves on the sweet gum turned deep red. Many leaves had fallen already, the sidewalk beneath the tree sprinkled with yellow and red blotches. In the spring, stains from those leaves would still be visible on the concrete.

Tennessee was all blue eyes and messy hair, her glow in-the-dark pajamas hiked to her knees and elbows, footnotes of restless sleep. She climbed from my lap down to the window and back to my lap several times, snuggling close. At the window, her light hair stuck to her forehead as she matched her face and hands to the prints on the glass. A Carolina wren sung loudly from the chain of the porch swing. Two titmice and a cardinal landed on the porch railings to pick at some fallen seeds. Tennessee pointed at the birds tufted crests and asked me to look at what she called the birds' *"hats"*.

I started a story for Tennessee, a fluid memory that hardened as I spoke: **"When I was nine, someone gave me my great-grandfather Howard's gray hat. It was shaped like this:"** I tried to describe it with my hands, roughly imitating the brim and the crease and the thin band around the base of the cap. Tennessee just looked at me, processed my hand signals as best as she could. She blinked and said nothing. I may as well have described soda pop to a wild rabbit and expected understanding.

My great-grandfather Howard died one morning while I was in elementary school. I don't remember even missing a class because of it. The family held the funeral on a weekend. My mother, brother, and I visited his body in an old church in Batavia, New York, a small town near where we lived with my mother at the time. The church smelled like books and feet, like a library. I remember that much. I also remember walking forward in my dark slacks and faded dress shoes and collared shirt and climbing the short step up to the coffin and looking in and wondering what you are supposed to do in these situations. I couldn't breathe correctly. There were people waiting for me to move, possibly even waiting for me to touch my palm to his room temperature face and to say something. I didn't say anything. I didn't touch him. I didn't move for a dozen seconds.

I couldn't say anything to him now even though I have had decades to think about what it means to look down on a dead ancestor. I feel nothing for this man, love or hate. I must acknowledge that, to me, certain relatives are simply meaningless. Most of us have that in common. We are related, Howard and I, sure, but we were not friends. We had tight genetics, but our genes also came to us mixed with the blood of mice and the cell walls of acorns. We formed beneath the constant push and pull of tides. We came from the atoms not yet smashed. None of that makes the relationship special. It just makes us a composition of ancient organics, and it makes me indifferent.

I have no useful stories about my great-grandfather, nothing of importance to pass on to Tennessee. If I don't care about this man, why should she? He was hard to understand, his throat always closed and dry. Our visits together in his assisted living apartment were brief, my mother doing most of the listening and all of the talking for us; I was a shallow presence.

Some months after that funeral, my maternal grandmother gave me the gray hat. A small remnant of a feather stuck in the outer band. The inside of the hat had a ring of smudged grease along the edge. I put it on. The brim came down over my eyes and ears. I took it off and put it away. Anything I know of Howard beyond that hat is invention. Did we ride together in a white car over the ruts of a winter cornfield? No, that was probably someone else. Wasn't he the one who taught me that you could eat dandelions? No, not him. Was it really his hat? I eventually lost track of it, and no one remembers me having it. He was a stranger, and when I talk about strangers, I don't need physical evidence to tell their stories. I can fill things in however I want, as is my right. A better story for Tennessee: ***"When I was nine I*** *found an old man's gray hat. It was shaped like this, and I got rid of it by throwing it into a brush fire."* A better lesson: why remember anything of insignificance.

    To invent a history about other people is all right, I guess. But what do I do with the stories I can never forget, like the night my ex-fiancé was drunk and confessed to cheating on me or that morning at the sink when I broke a butter dish and it prompted my father to speak quietly about his brother killing himself? These are my stories, but I don't know if my children will need them. Will they care if my father grew up in a house near a horse-chestnut tree that dropped shiny, poisonous seeds? Or that I used to pick up those seeds and select one to drop into my front pocket and rub the skin of it with my thumb until the whorls on that finger were dirty and red from the pressure I exerted? My father told me never to eat the seeds, but sometimes I would lick my fingers after handling them. I don't know why. Maybe just to see if what he told me was true. Was it? Would you lick your fingers, Tennessee?

    That tree and house are gone now. I can only tell stories since horse-chestnut trees don't grow in the south where I now live. Instead, we have sweet gums. I can say to my curious children, *"Yes, horse-chestnuts exist. You can look it up in a guidebook. Someday you may brush your hands against its scratchy bark. But you haven't seen it yet with your own eyes, you haven't been able to hold its seeds and darken your thumb because you have not been near enough to one to grab it. Let me tell you about my parents, about our house on wheels, about fireflies trapped in glass jars."*

*****

I was five years old when my parents split in 1979, my brother only three. That year, the divorce rate in the US peaked. Statistically our situation was far from special in any way, but that does not make our family's place among the data any less miserable.

As for why it happened, the simplest and clearest reason is that my mother cheated. There may have been other reasons like my father's drinking or financial worries or general incompatibility, but the infidelity put all the other explanations to the side. To make things worse, the person she took up with was a womanizing divorcee whose first wife—according to my grandparents—had had enough of him only after he threw her down a set of stairs and broke several of her bones. This man would became my stepfather, but he established his power and cruelty long before that formality occurred. She divorced him too, twenty years too late. To be with this abuser, she destroyed our family.

Nearly four decades later, my mother doesn't want to talk about the split or the reasons for it, in fact have never spoken about it in anything but vague or defensive terms. I may never get an answer from her to the question that I put forth: What went wrong? She knows I know about the adultery. She would need to start her story from a vulnerable position, which makes it that much harder to say the words.

My father was much the opposite. In my experience, the wronged person in a relationship tends to be more open about what happened. When my brother and I were growing up my father often spoke about what he and our mother would be doing at such and such a time if they were still together. Maybe they paid the house off. Or maybe they paid it off twenty years before, bought an RV and drove to all the national parks. They may have had a third child.

One thing he was sure of was that we kids would have had the upbringing and stability that we deserved. But instead, as he told me more than once, *"She just came to me one day and said I don't love you anymore and that was it. There was nothing I could do. Ten years of marriage, poof. Back then it was rare for the father to get custody, so she took you kids, and I got nothing."*

This single event shaped my entire life, the fracture. The hole still feels open in me. I climb into that hole during sleepless nights when my tired mind breaks free from reality, and I get stuck awake and thinking awful thoughts—ways that I might die, ways my children might die, what would I do if something happened to my partner Kristin. The thoughts in that hole are irrational and ornate. I imagine things like a car crashing into the house and smashing into our bedroom, bullets falling through the ceiling after a round of celebratory gunshots in the neighborhood, bizarre accidents involving power lines and bicycles. Once I get into this cycle, it takes me a long time to settle. When I climb from the hole, I move on to thinking of more realistic ways my family could dissolve. I know that I could not endure what my father went through. But what would happen if things were reversed, if it was I that left in some way?

*****

Summer solstice in Durham and the sparrows have already reared their second brood. Our own second child Hazel is four weeks old. Hazel nestles at Kristin's neck as she shushes and hums and sways in the porch swing. Tennessee and I walk through the front yard looking at insects moving in the grass. As we walk, she collects a thick bouquet of long dandelion stems and swings the bundle around her face and sides, the heads of each stem releasing white fluffy seeds from tiny sockets. The seeds drift in all directions, into her hair, onto her clothing. She laughs when the fluff tickles her face.

I sit down on the front steps and watch Tennessee continue to play in the yard. Across the street in the bright sweet-gum tree, catbirds mewl like sick infants. To my right, two robins clutch the top of the chain link fence, their beaks full of worms that wiggle like living beards. Starlings move through the yard like wind-up toys: step step peck, step step peck, step step stop. The cardinals scavenge along the ground below the bird feeders in search of oily sunflower seeds. Beside us are more dandelions ready for picking, ready for their seeds to release. Everything around us is lively and optimistic, motivated by the instinct to reproduce and to thrive.

Humans are different. We mix our instincts with modern desire, pleasure, and a capacity to flee. When Kristin has a hard time getting Hazel to breast-feed, she wonders how there are so many people in this world if this simple act of feeding an infant is so difficult. I agree. I nod. I utter assurances. But the parental bond itself is difficult. After the sleep stunted nights and the crying and the shitty diapers, my first thought is not to love but to run, to slam doors and dart into the street to find a stranger with a fast car and a blank, silent face. In this way I become more like my mother. Perhaps I get in that fast car and understand what she needed.

Starting a family is risky with constant opportunities to lose everything or wear down the bonds of affection and attraction that exist between two humans in love. I think about losing it all, about suddenly being alone. What would it be like to have only memories of Kristin's body above mine, merged, warm, and thinking of the passing of seconds, not lifetimes? What if we never again lay together naked and content, hands and arms and legs tangled in chaotic, wilted arrangements? What if the only remaining connection we held was that of distant, bitter children? If Tennessee or Hazel sat across from me and I held and bounced my grandchild at the table, what would I tell them about how things fell apart? Those thoughts make me reach out to touch Kristin while she sleeps and won't remember, make me hug my children and tell them how the birds live, how their parents and the cardinals call this place home all year round.

Part Two:
Poetry Chapbooks

mus·cled
mus·cu·lar
mus·cu·lar·is
mus·cu·lar·i·ty
 pl mus·cu·lar·i·ties
mus·cu·lar·ly
mus·cu·la·tion
mus·cu·la·ture
mus·cu·lo·apo·
 neu·rot·ic
mus·cu·lo·cu·ta·
 ne·ous
mus·cu·lo·mem·
 bra·nous
mus·cu·lo·phren·
 ic
mus·cu·lo·skel·e·
 tal
mus·cu·lo·spi·ral
mus·cu·lo·ten·di·
 nous
mus·cu·lo·trop·ic
mus·cu·lus
 pl mus·cu·li
nu·sen·na
 also me·sen·na
 or mous·sena
nush·room
nu·si·co·ther·a·
 py
 pl mu·si·co·ther·a·
 pies
nus·si·ta·tion
nus·tard
nu·ta·fa·cient
nu·ta·gen

pl mu·ta·gen·e·ses
mu·ta·gen·ic
mu·ta·gen·i·cal·ly
mu·ta·ge·nic·i·ty
 pl mu·ta·ge·nic·i·ties
mu·tant
mu·ta·ro·tase
mu·ta·ro·ta·tion
mu·tase
mu·tate
 mu·tat·ed
 mu·tat·ing
mu·ta·tion
mu·ta·tion·al
mu·ta·tion·al·ly
mu·ta·tor
mu·ti·late
 mu·ti·lat·ed
 mu·ti·lat·ing
mu·ti·la·tion
mu·ti·la·tor
mu·tism
mu·tu·al·ism
mu·tu·al·ist
muz·zle
 muz·zled
 muz·zling
my·al·gia
my·al·gic
my·as·the·nia
my·as·the·nia
 grav·is
my·as·then·ic
my·a·to·nia
 muscular flabbiness
 (*see* myotonia)

my·ce·li·o
my·ce·li·u
 pl my·ce·li·
my·ce·tisn
my·ce·tis·
 pl my·ce·ti
my·ce·to·g
my·ce·toid
my·ce·to·n
 pl my·ce·to
 or my·ce·to
My·ce·to·z
my·ce·to·z
My·co·bac·
 ce·ae
my·co·bac·
my·co·bac·
 sis
 pl my·co·ba
 ses
my·co·bac·
 um
 pl my·co·ba
my·co·cide
My·co·der
my·co·der·
 toid
 or my·co·de
 tous
my·col·ic
my·co·log·i
 also my·co·l
my·co·log·i
 ly
my·col·o·gi
my·col·o·gy
 pl my·col·o·g

gravity kills

#1

There is always a chance that

    we will fall.

That is just the nature of it.

    Gravity kills.

In Memoriam

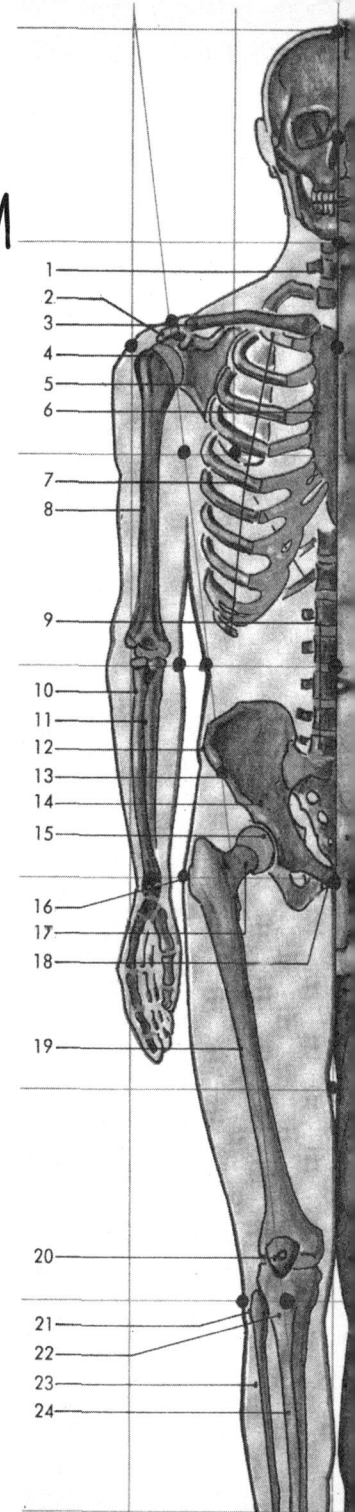

I

Scan the names
Lives in bold
Loving mother, wife

Fingers blackened
By fresh newsprint

II

For commonality; Carbon
Oxygen, Hydrogen
And this, your Arsenic

III

Pine; Velvet;
Grief
No one noticed
I stole your wedding ring

HOMELESS

You look at him,
his sickly head
stuck to shoulders
like an ant covered
lollipop
morphing on concrete.
His face sweet
but never touched
by pet's breath
or aftershave
or even the vapid steps
of moonless walks.
He divines in puddle water
and pigeon leaves,
walking chestnut
covered streets
in a world
made bitter
by even numbers
and pockets
without change.
You look at him
as he asks your name
your words swift,
staggered,
and vomited to the shadows
as the lamps
map the wet pavement.

The Warbler

When I had snapped a twig from a black birch,
And set the flavor of its blood upon my tongue,
I heard the Yellowthroat's rapid chant
Descend upon me.

Witchity-witchity-witchity-witch

As the bird passed,
I heard the muffled clap of warbler hands -
An ovation for the morning sun.
I followed the bird
past the fallen heroes
of an oak's battle for the sky

The song in repose,
I rest near the stream that feeds the warbler,
Hoping to glimpse a thrush nest
Buried in its veiny bank.
The flash of brook trout
Steals my wonder
and I find myself asking aloud
about the intertwined contraptions
of evolution and fate.

The Stream

I could watch the stream
Cooling my feet,
The foaming water
Still moving towards
Its end.

I might snatch a few stones
From her belly,
Capture the end
In my mind -
Snap the middle in silver,
Hang it on my wall,
Tell the story to my guests
As they dine on baked Brie,
And run their fingers
Over the organs
I stole from that far off body.

Or I may simply stay home,
Buy a book on Falling Water,
pretend
I loved that part
Of Pennsylvania -
Its long winded Waterthrush
Watching the sun move over
Land laced with fences,
Knowing that their fellows
Sing no notes of 'master'.

Roaches

Outside, I put boot prints on the roaches
and leave them on the sidewalk
for the birds to pick at.
At home, I'll beat them
with a worn copy of some book (I forget the title),
and kick the carcass across
the pine floor. Maybe watch the dog chase it.
He seems too old or indifferent to chase the live ones.
Me too. A symptom of life and acquiring life's debt.
We chase the dead,
and leave the living for the young.
I believe it. I don't like it. It makes me
think about my own kind of sidewalk,
and the life that will leave me
for the roaches to pick at.

Planning

We always take it for granted
that someone else
will take the bullet
while we make our own plans
do you think that the kid
shot on 30th Street
last Sunday
didn't have plans?
What about those people
on the plane?
They were planning to do something
but they ended up
in a cornfield in Alamance County
North Carolina

Captain Cook

I like my bar stools
To bear me uneasily
So I can tap along
To the staccato
Of conversation.

I like my bartenders
To engage me for awhile -
Tell me
What they have learned
From the other bar stools.

I like to nod and say
I did not know
Captain Cook
Died in Hawaii.

Directions

Take a right at the Church of Christ,
continue running until you see the motel
where the bathroom near the front desk
has a toilet seat embossed by boot prints
inked by salt and slop from a walkway
                    cleared of ice.

Slow down and pass behind two men
smoking cigarettes in a shadow
as quietly as two pillows touching.
Stop and listen; a killdeer repeats in an evening
blurred parking lot where the lights
are busy or insipid or blown
                    out with bullets.

Turn left at the oak tree, the one
with the gash at the base growing
mushrooms yellow and low and wet
like a cat's vomit. There is a cardboard
sign in the grass that says "homles, living in
forst, NEthing helps" near where a school
bus ran a red light one morning;
                    nothing bad happened.

Stain

Our bare heels are stained

      blue

black

        with mulberries fallen ripe.

Baby #2

Day 1: We haven't settled on the name,
and I don't understand how this skin-
to-skin thing is comfortable for this child
brushing against all this wiry hair
on my chest.

Day 3: Skin is peeling around his eyelids,
unfurling like old wallpaper from the edge
of the baseboard. It is fascinating to tug
pieces off the sleeping child and ball
the bits in my fingers.

Day 6: We all smell like sour milk.

Day 7: On a trip to the pharmacy, we
bump into people with the cart.
"Sorry about that. No wait…
I don't actually care."

Day 9: I think I brushed my teeth twice
today.

Day 11: Our older kid pissed on the floor and
asked me what I was going to do about it,
partly mocking, partly making a serious inquiry.
I tell her I'll probably just clean it up then
go back to quickly ingesting black coffee.

Day 12: No matter where you plant cabbage
    the cabbage moths will come. You will see the
    white wings from the kitchen window and
    remember that the black shirt you have on is
    crusty with vomit.

Day 14: The house smells like vinegar pickles.
    And shit. Pickles and baby shit.

Day 15: We all smell like yeast.

Day 17: I can't fucking stop fucking humming.

Day 18: At the park I watch a formation
    of gnats near the ground, hundreds of
    flying flashes, individuals coming together into
    the shapes of human organs and balloons.
    The cluster disbands when a child
    walks through it, spitting, clutching her nose.
    Collections of green tulip poplar leaves dot the
    ground, little islands in the dark mulch.

Day 19: I watch a house fly walk on the window.
    I ask out loud why insects need blood. Cicadas
    scream above the laundry I hung two days ago
    and forgot about while I burnt dinner.

Day 24: I wonder what balance of nature is
    disturbed when a spacecraft full of rare
    Earth metals is launched into the ether,
    never to return. I remind myself that
    five tons of steel weighs the same
    as five tons of feathers.

House Sparrow

There are house sparrows bathing in the water fountains at JFK airport. A few people pass by the birds and make comments that I cannot hear. Most people simply ignore the birds and continue on to their gates or off to baggage claim or to a car waiting in long term parking. No one bothers to get the birds out of the fountains. The birds move when someone comes in for a drink but come right back when the space clears out. It seems that no one is in charge of getting rid of the birds. No one is accountable to that task. So the birds move from fountain to roof beam and back, shitting into the food court that opens up to the skylights. I get a drink at the fountain; the nozzle has a ring of purple lipstick.

**

From the plane window the swimming pools look like those little round containers that hold watercolor paints. There are gardens against the pools, which look orderly from above but are most likely run through with wiregrass and lambs-quarter and ant mounds. There is no way to tell what is growing and what is dead, only that there are spaced rows and those rows are contained by green grass and fences.

**

Across the street—a winding, two lane road through the Vermont mountains—the meadow is full of golden rod. I cannot make out anything else, the yellow is too vibrant. A mowed trail cuts through the yellow; it is someone's job to keep the path walkable. Right now rain comes straight down and hits all those yellow flowers. The color won't wash off. Cars pass, slowing down as the rain comes faster.

**

What anyone does with what they know is probably nobody's business, but we cannot do much or go anywhere without the aid of a person or persons applying what they know in some manner or another. The bus runs because people built it, maintain it and know how to drive it. People are buried because that was their last wish and other people know how to dig holes and lower big boxes full of remains into the open soil.

**

House sparrows were introduced into the Americas by Europeans who wished to recreate the sights and sounds of their birthplaces. The male sparrows are "strikingly patterned" according to the guidebooks, white cheeks and black throat contrasting to a mostly brown body. The females are considered drab in comparison. This applies to much of the bird world, a sexual division of what humans describe as striking and what is not striking. This description ignores that both sexes can fly.

House sparrows constantly speak to each other. Ornithologists attempt to use our alphabet to recreate, in visual form, the sounds birds make. So the chips and squeaks of the house sparrow become *seeadit* and *chew-chew* and *ch'wuh-tit*. How to pronounce the apostrophe is not addressed in the field guides, so a birder must listen for a space, a pause that is brief yet somehow remarkable enough to become a symbol in bird speech. *Apostrophe as space.*

**

I get closer to the meadow and the yellow dominance of the golden rod begins to part into patches of milkweed and crimson clover; Queen Anne's lace gone to seed, brittle and brown; morning glory vines placing their white, tuba shaped flowers on top of vetch and short grasses. The milkweed pods are just beginning to plump. Bull thistle patches rise up from the green with bright purple flowers, full and insect covered, smelling like that summer in Elba, at home, the last summer I ever spent in New York.

Flies

The flies in the mudroom are big as bolt heads, black.
They crawl up through the cracks in the unfinished floor,
its jagged edges of thick, darkening plywood
well gapped for travel of insects, smells.

Rats died in the basement
from green cubed poison thrown
into the dampness
through an access
door no larger than my crumpled body.

Rats died in the basement,
converted into these thick black flies, lots of them,
big and slow.

BABY #1

I am tired of pacing with the newborn. I put the bathroom fan on for white noise, shut the two of us in that small space. I pat his back with a cupped palm. The sound is a muffled drum:

> *thump thump thump* a rhythm, heartbeat as tempo.

One two three, one two three. I whisper and shush.

I fade with the screaming, the wiggling, the weight of this slight human

> increasing .

I think of days and nights with no kids, staying up and drinking until the yawning would not quit. I can taste beer right then, in this parenthood, in a dim bathroom with the fan above and the smell of urine in the unflushed toilet.

Swing Shift

At the boot factory, we played Euchre at lunch,
smoked cigarettes clean to the filter.
I set boxes into hot dark trailers
bound for Ontario, collected soda cans
from trash cans near the time clock
adding nickels to swing shift pay.

**

There is a water leak in the crawlspace,
the outer brick façade of the foundation
broken from a sledgehammer strike,
a crude attempt at a fix or an attempt at a viewing.
I can hear the leak when I pass by,
a hiss like a child mimicking a snake,
mimicking the rain,
mimicking the ocean.
The sidewalk makes a poor container;
seepage polishes the granite curb
wet and shiny like ice.

**

Near the top of the dumpster, apples,
one green pepper with a hole near the middle,
several lemons and limes browned where bloom
once met stem. We made applesauce
with too much cinnamon.

Part Three:
Essays and Flash Nonfiction

Briggs Avenue is adapted from *Quitter #8*

Briggs Avenue

Mid-summer and the rain approaches without much warning. The wind comes up first, sucks a bit of the humidity from the air, and cools things down. It is only late afternoon, but the streetlights pop on after the first heavy clouds move in to drape the sky. Traffic outside calms then disappears as the rain falls fast, a gray curtain. The rain is thick. It hangs like rope connecting soil and sky, makes seeing the house across the street nearly impossible. We sit in the living room, each of us watching the storm in our own way.

Lightning runs along a tree down the street. The strike isn't terribly close; I couldn't hear that particular electric buzzing. But the thunder comes right on top of the flash. It is loud like a train passing through the house. The cats scatter, their nails digging into the wood floor as best they can. The house shakes, dishes vibrate in the stainless steel sink. Tennessee drops the book she was looking through and runs to me. I sit in the rocking chair, looking out onto the street. We were all talking about the amount of water coming off the roof until right up to jolt, how we couldn't wait until the new gutters and roof got installed. Tennessee hugs my neck tight and the three of us go silent. The rest of the storm moves through quickly, all the thunder becoming distant and muted.

Post-storm yellow light enters the house. Raindrops along the edges of the storm windows invert the world and become tiny depictions of reflected reality. I watch as that pale and bright yellow gives way to dull green and eventually to the purple of an urban evening. The street lights stay on, hold the night off, hold us all in. After the storm I am scared of what can reach us out in the darkness. Tennessee slides down from my lap, grabs one of her stuffed animals and wraps it in a small blanket. She talks to it as she carries it from her mother to me and back again.

Tennessee goes still as she leans against the couch where Kristin sits. *"You lost your baby, Mama?"*

Kristin removes her eyes from the window and looks at me while she answers, without hesitation or sigh, *"Yes sweet'ums. But someday there might be another one."*

*****

The morning after the storm, I look out the divided window of our back door. I don't blink. My lips are dry and fastened in a tight line across my face. A taut wire clothesline runs through my stare. Wooden clothespins clasp the otherwise empty wire. They are aging out there in the elements, darkening and staining with a subtly fragrant mildew. I count the pins slowly and silently. I try to take my time, but I get distracted by the line itself. The green plastic coating of the wire is wet with dew. Small drops of moisture form like pimples along its length. I start counting all over again and try to really focus my attention on this impossibly simple task. Once, twice; I stop only when I get the same count three times in a row. This is as close as I come to meditation. It isn't working.

Grackles move around the pokeweed that grows thick near the fence line. The birds' greasy metallic backs and tails always look wet and slick liked waxed fruit. They squeak and whistle amongst each other as I grab the handle of the door. The birds quickly fly off, pulling their grouping back together somewhere farther down the street. Other birds stay and wait; a fledgling mockingbird clings to the top rung of the fence. It is guarded and fattened by each of its parents, one of them feeding the child while the other yells into the yard. The shrieking bird spreads its wings in a threat to something beyond my narrowing vision, something that means nothing to me because I cannot see it.

I slap my face hard. One slap, three slaps, no use counting anymore, just hit me. Can I even describe what this is like, this knowledge that sadness is coming for me, and there is nothing that I can do to stop it? Even this physically violent method does nothing to disperse the coming storm. I am lightning connecting with a transformer on a pole; I am a race horse that just broke its leg. There is no stopping what has happened from linking with what will happen. I stop hitting myself and count the clothespins for a fourth time. I force myself to know that I am loved, that this disease can surface from time to time and I can get through it with just that basic knowledge, that understanding that someone inside this house cares whether or not I exist. I mutter it to myself: Someone needs me.

A chain link fence squares off our backyard. Sections of the fence are buckled from old injuries, indentations from where tree branches fell and snapped in pieces. The branches are long gone. A young, thin pecan tree rises near the edge of the fence. Several of its branch tips are covered in the gray tents of webworms. Hundreds of orange headed worms will eventually drop to the ground to pupate in the fall. White moths will rise from the leaf cover and proceed with a life cycle that is easily observed. When we were kids, my brother and I would spray the lower tents with hairspray and light it all on fire. The worms would smoke and wiggle and pop in the flames. They would plunge to the ground like burning rain, and we would stomp them thoroughly like there was nothing else to do.

Tennessee finds me at the door. After a few moments of back and forth with her, I open it, and we leave the house and hurry out into the yard. A children's moon rests over our shoulders, a gray and flat disk passing in and out of the valleys of a few mountainous clouds. The sky is otherwise light and pale blue, reassuring. We come out here because, as I stood at the door slapping and muttering to myself, Tennessee came up behind me and made a fuss about wanting to pee in the grass. We have no problem with her doing it. We just want her to do it in the backyard.

"Ten, you can't pee in the front yard right now. You have to wait until after the complete collapse of society makes it acceptable."

"You promise?"

"I promise. Until then, only in the backyard."

Like me, she enjoys this feral act of letting go. I was raised in the country and could piss wherever I wanted. My father was the lead to follow in this regard. Whenever I visit his house, I piss on the barn just like I did as a kid. This act helps me recall that I am part of something much broader than myself; no matter how deeply I get buried emotionally, no matter where I happen to be physically, within me there will always be nutrition for something else.

After my parents split up, I lived with my mother and brother on a busy road near town. We only lived there for a short period of time. It was a stopover for us, a cheap duplex with cable television and bunk beds. The busy road did not deter me from pissing outside. One morning as I peed on the cement blocks of the foundation underneath the kitchen window, I looked up to see my mother and her new boyfriend looking down at me, faces furrowed deep with anger.

"What's the big deal?" was all I could think to say. After I went inside and when my mother wasn't looking, her boyfriend (my future step-father) hit me hard on the back of the head.

*****

Tennessee digs her fingernails into the green outer hull of a pecan that fell from our tree. It fell before the nut inside was ready. After ten minutes of scraping the edges and tips of the hull, her fingers and palms have turned a sickly yellow. She holds her right hand to my ear because she has discovered that her sticky hand makes a slight noise as she unfurls her fist. I take her hand gently and look it over. The space under the tips of her nails is stained black like she has done nothing with her time on this planet other than dig barehanded in thick, rich soil. The lines of her palm are darker than the rest, the crevices of the folds holding harder to the stain. I take her hand in mine, ball her fist within my fist and press it all to my forehead. I close my eyes and envision that I am connecting to the ground through my child, imagining I can somehow travel through her and bury the coming sickness underground among the roots and the larvae and the constant dampness.

"Can you step on this, Papa?" She asks me to crush a pecan under the heel of my shoe. I comply. She fetches more. A greasy wet streak forms where I press my weight down

on each nut, smashing it into the concrete patio. The smell that rises as the unripe nuts come apart is strong and green like raw firewood. Tennessee keeps the pecans coming, and I keep crushing them until the concrete is frothy with the natural oil and water that emerges from the seeds.

A small pile of nut meat and sharp shell fragments builds on the patio. I tell her that I am done crushing for now, that I just want to sit here and look out into the fence line and try to breathe deeply and correctly. I want to sort myself out as my vision continues to narrow and tremble. But she doesn't understand how to stop moving, how to stop learning and receiving information, how to just take all the material and sort it into neat stacks of knowledge. She convinces me to stand up from the chair to look closely at what we have done together. I find it ugly and gross. Tennessee puts her hands into the pile and squeezes.

A squirrel runs up the tree behind us and out into the branches high above. The scratch of claws on bark is unmistakable. The squawk that follows as the creature calls out warnings to its peers is also distinct. Leaves fall as the animal crosses the expanse and jumps to another tree. I swear at the squirrel under my breath for no reason other than it seems like the sensible thing to do. These are the weird and brief moments when I think I can still mitigate and challenge what is happening by deflection and self-control. I am running out of ideas.

"Do you hear that squirrel, Ten?"

"What's that squirrel saying, Papa?"

"I don't know. It seems unhappy with something, maybe unhappy with us."

The squirrel's noise stops. There is a temporary silence as we kick and throw the nut pieces out into the grass below the clothesline. By evening all the good pieces will be gone as the critters come out and lay claims among the clover and wiregrass of the yard. The mice and the birds and the opossum all have their moments when they are alone and can appreciate all this smashing I did with the heel of my foot.

A block away, the siren of a fire truck starts up and all the neighborhood dogs begin to howl along. Tennessee giggles. I focus on the dogs' reactions without thinking of the tragedy beyond the siren—the highway accident, the house on fire, the body in the street. My emotional connections are rerouted or broken. I breathe lazily through my slightly open mouth and just stare at the ugly, rusting, and intertwined diamonds of the chain-link fence.

Tennessee hugs my leg again, and I feel nothing, shake her off. Petty and unreasonable irritation builds. I sigh hard, groan harder, grab my face with both hands and push up from chin to temple over and over again. The sound of my rough hands on the stubble of my face is sharp and familiar, but it isn't familiar enough to ground me. I am in too deep; there is nothing more for me to do than go lie down and sleep through the worst of it, rise in the morning and continue taking the medications that thankfully make these instances short lived.

*****

Tennessee wakes from a bad dream. Her cries wake us. Kristin and I roll over to face her and calm her in the darkness of the room. She can't put her words together to explain what went wrong. We try the usual lines—*"Everything is OK, sweet one. Mama and Papa are right here. What's wrong, sweet'ums?"*—but there is nothing we can offer her except diversion. Diversion is familiar, something I know a lot about. I sleepily ask her about a book we were reading before bedtime, and she instantly becomes silent and then talkative, but serious.

"Bears don't ride bikes, Papa." We talk it out for a few minutes and she is calm and yawning and welcoming the pillow as she lies back down. I am jealous and wishing I was so easily distracted and mollified.

I can't go back to sleep. I think about the dream I just had where Tennessee saw my long dead grandfather. He had a line of children, grandchildren and great-grandchildren all waiting in a line to see him and meet him as he sat still on a couch. Everyone was crying, myself included. It was that hard and cathartic dream sobbing that I have sometimes. It was a chance for me to just dump sadness like a heavy bucket of water that had no place to go, no growing tree to nourish.

In the dream, everyone came to realize that my grandfather was dead. We prepared to carry out his dying wish, which he had written on a large piece of paper on the floor. It said, *"I want you to burn this house down with me in it."* I woke up just after we had crumpled a bunch of newspapers and phone book pages under the coffee table and sparked up a lighter.

Whenever I wake up in the night, I look in Tennessee's direction and find the lump of her tiny body among the blankets and stuffed animals. I reach my hand for her head and leave it there for a moment before moving down to her ribcage. In the otherwise still darkness I wait for her breathing to move my hand up and down a few times. This touch is a reassurance before I go back to sleep, a little ritual to make sure that she is there and alive and safe. It is also another way of grounding myself, observing the reality of this love right there beside me.

I want her to know, almost unconsciously, that if she has the same problems that I have that I won't leave her to figure them out on her own. My hand will be there for her, helping her press back against the weight. She will come to understand that there is nothing more sinister or beautiful than genetic inheritance. It is strong and robust but also callous, unsympathetic and oblivious. Because of that, the same disease of depression that has a hold of me may exist within her.

No hard feelings, Tennessee, but this is you now, this is how you got zipped together, how the atoms aligned. Nothing I do can change that; we all take these chances when we decide to reproduce.

Tennessee may want answers to why she feels this way or that way, why she can't seem to shake sadness on otherwise warm and sunny days. Just as I did, she will want to know what the problem is, if it is natural or if things will ever be different. She will want to know if she can fight through it like a tiger at the throat of its prey, or if it is best to just wait it out, deal with it as best she can at that moment and not delay in seeking treatment.

Whenever I can, whenever she might be able to understand, I'll tell her, *"Tennessee, I am sorry about the burdens, but I wanted so badly for you to be here."*

Thin

Six thirty in the morning and everything has a misty haze around it, thin and blue. I cross a sleeping road and shuffle up a graveled tractor trail to enter the forest. I walk along the thick overhangs of a stream where the roots of beech trees are exposed and gnarled like arthritic fingers. The stream bank levels out at the first ford. There the water is thin and pure. It reminds me of peach skin, something juicy. Above, new leaves wait to open on the skeletal trees. Last year's leaves and twigs cover the path that interrupts the guts of the forest, those darkening innards seldom traveled by humans. Sound amplifies in the leafless air. Breath comes out visible; the fogged air sticks to my clothing like transparent adhesive tape. Droplets of the morning's mist stand out on the fibers of my jacket. The sun will dry the jacket later, but now, in the close darkness of dawn, it looks as if thousands of tiny, translucent lollipops cover me.

Viscera is adapted from *Quitter #7*

Viscera

I was ten years old the first time I butchered an animal. It was early winter, the sun low and cold. I huffed from running after the beagles as they chased a rabbit. The dogs howled as they ran, spreading away from me, galloping feet tracing lines in the snow. I fired once at the rabbit as it crossed to my side. The ear ringing mark of the shotgun echoed among the maples and oaks, long clear of leaves. I ejected the shell, took in the metallic whisper of it. I stood sniffling from the cold, looking at the lump of gray fur that no longer moved. My stepfather came behind me as I stepped silently towards the rabbit.

I wedged the rabbit's head into the crotch of a tree branch as my stepfather growled instructions. He was a cruel man, always ready to raise his voice and hands. This is the man who kicked my brother in the stomach for forgetting to flush the toilet, who threw me down a set of concrete steps for raking leaves incorrectly, who left bruises the size of oranges just below my mother's elbows from where he grabbed her and forced her to answer to a slight. Out there among the brambles in the squat forest, he smacked the back of my head and pointed to where I should make the first cut.

I didn't say prayers at the butchering, didn't offer thanks. I didn't think I needed to. My stepfather said it was only a rabbit. Earlier that morning, as I walked the forest on my own, I shot a white-throated sparrow for no reason. I took aim and blasted the small bird into fluff as it perched in a thicket. I had imagined, briefly, that the bird was my stepfather's eye.

YOU AND I

I brush my teeth and blood **pours out.** It is Sunday morning. I make coffee so black that I think of gravity wells and astrophysics and the long orbits of asteroids. I skip breakfast. I almost always skip breakfast. On Sunday I am the last one to wake. I get an hour or two with the bedroom all to myself. The curtains are drawn tight at night to keep the streetlight from entering our unconsciousness. But the curtains keep the room dark even as our tiny place in the world enters into view of the sun. When I wake up there is no way to know the weather, and that is both good and bad. If the sun is abundant and the air perfectly still and warm, I come to hate that I have slept so late and haven't been outside to hear the earliest of the birds and their blanket of song. If it is raining and cold then I don't mind as much that I have gone back to sleep. No matter the weather, I think about the extra hours I lay there, the time I have lost being with my family.

A long time ago, in between relationships, I would have spent the weekend in bed, alone in my tiny apartment, rising only to go to the fridge and get beer or open the cupboards looking for that cheap Scotch with the label that should just say REGRET. That's the life, eh? Stinking and drunk and hopeless about where isn't and what won't and who didn't. I would grab the mirror of the bathroom medicine cabinet and look into cloudy, disabled eyes, staring into this thing, my life. I have suffered from depression for most of my life, even when I didn't have the words to say what it was. When I drank it would be alright for the night, but I would be crippled again by morning.

In a dream I can sometimes tell myself it is just a dream and then do whatever I want. That is lucid dreaming, but lucid reality has things like getting out of bed and paying bills and finding the desire to eat something. We can't talk ourselves out of that reality. It is a highway with no exits. We just have to realize that sometimes you just have to yank the wheel and cross the median and slam right into what is coming from the other direction. But holy fucking shit, who would do that? Who could do that? Trust me to make that decision and that trust is misplaced. Trust me to go to counseling or keep up with medication or quit drinking and you better be ready for some hand holding and finger pointing and dodging of clenched fists.

I am talking to myself, about myself, a conversation about how you know when things are at a point when even stuffy and damp darkness is better than cool and breezy light. "I can't help you. I don't know how. Most importantly I don't know why I would." That's where I would start this conversation. My—our—problem is not unique. We have a common disease, you and I—younger me and older me—and the problem is that we now know that we have it but we can't ever talk ourselves out of it. We stick to our medications, but there are still times when noon comes and something goes wrong with work or the garbage bag breaks open in the kitchen or nothing actually happens at all and we can feel the sadness come from our guts and spread like summer kudzu. We start pacing. We hiss *fuck fuck fuck* through clenched teeth. We rub our face from chin to neck hoping to pull this thing out of us like venom. We think about our children and how to tell them about this and that—especially that—and tell them of those nights and days we spent not moving like we were already dead.

Hot & Cold

There is a moist morning light, a vapored orange glow just behind the full leafed trees. It is the kind of light that makes a poet pause and walk slowly. But it is also a sign of heat, another reason to walk slow. The air is sticky. Sweat is already on my back and forming a damp ridge just above my first ribs. My gray shirt darkens there. A line forms, a blob actually, tying together small spots into a larger shape. It doesn't look like anything recognizable like a snake or a row of pears, at least not from my angle of view. It is simply the imprint of a hot day. That is all the shape it holds.

    A train horn sounds off wild and brilliant to the north of me. The horn becomes louder and more frantic as the train moves through intersections, gates coming down over pavement like slow, dull guillotines as their own clangs mingle with those of the train. The noise of the freight wheels click along, that constant metronome staccato and those unanticipated squeals. I imagine the box cars both plain and vandalized and full of things that fit well together inside something that size. Even through the blanket of cicada and cricket noise I can hear the sound. It doesn't remind me of anything in particular except maybe rust and gravel, two things that no train will ever be rid of.

Folk science says you can tell the temperature on a summer day by counting the number of cricket chirps that happen in thirteen seconds and adding forty to that number. I try it, but it doesn't give me anything accurate. I force myself to really listen, to isolate a single calling male out here in the weeds. I can't do it.

*****

The cabin is quiet and dark. I turn on the lamp near the fireplace and squint my eyes in the new light. The lamp has a bare bulb; everything is all harsh contrast and shadow until I can get to the light above the kitchen sink. That fluorescent light slowly comes alive, a hum and buzz as the electrons get their breakfast of alternating current. Under this light my hands and arms are a sickly color and the porcelain sink looks dirty and yellow. Two dying crickets twitch at the bottom of the sink. Their presence reminds me to check the mousetraps near the oven.

This is my morning ritual: wake up in the dark, sweaty in my sleeping bag; unzip myself and gently place my feet onto the cold floor of the cabin; walk to the lights; check the mouse traps; dress quickly and walk out into the cold. These are the movements I make as the sun remains buried below the horizon. The sun has risen and set over half of the world by now. While I wake up and walk out into the forest, other people are just now nodding off to sleep or eating dinner or pacing silently with their arms crossed in front of their chest, walking with determination towards no determined end, waiting for a resolution for the anxiety that grips every single one of us.

It is helpful for me to know that off somewhere in every direction, the subways and trains are running already and have been all night. Freight is stacked high on container ships that are moving from port to port, slicing through ocean waves whether I wake up or not. There are planes in the sky right now, in the darkness above me. Some window shades on the plane are drawn and a few reading lights are switched on; someone is ordering a second cup of coffee and trying to figure out a six letter word for *"first among siblings"*. All those people and things, all those stories out there that have nothing to do with me or this place in the middle of the woods in Pennsylvania, cold and dark now even though our shared sun is working its way to me.

Blood Moon

Six in the morning and the lunar eclipse is low in the west and red. I stand outside the warehouse where I work and watch a truck arrive at the gates of a neighboring building. A group of three teens walk past me in the muted darkness on their way to school, their chests and faces lit with the light from their phones. They don't look up at the moon. They don't see me looking at the moon. They don't ask what I am doing looking at the moon. The moon is just up there, a vertical slice of brightness squinting down on us like a snake eye. I watch as the sliver of light on the moon becomes smaller. I run inside to pour my coffee, but get distracted with other things. By the time I get back outside, the moon is too low in the sky for me to see. I missed the blood moon, again.

 I sit down at my desk and begin the day, the sky just beginning to brighten. Across the street and across the railroad tracks, the grapple excavator at the scrap yard comes alive. The fence around it hides its cargo until it lifts above my line of sight. Cars, aluminum siding, stoves, buses, massive tangles of wire all come up from below the fence like fish into a boat. The grapple claw dumps the metal into railway cars and presses the mass down with its immense jaw. This is a giant of metal itself, a cannibal. As long as it is somewhat light out, the claw is working. It never stops.

Blur

It is late afternoon and the clouds are thin and shapeless. It is the time of year when the sidewalks downtown are dotted with little brown mounds. The mounds are cedar waxwings, drunk on the fermenting berries of yaupon and cedar, and flying into the clear windows of tall buildings. Some are stunned; most are dead. I myself am so drunk that I have forgotten where I parked my car. I am convinced that someone has stolen it. I walk ten blocks north to the police station to file a report.

"What color is it? Do you know the license plate number?"

I rub my lips with the edge of a forefinger, rolling off a thin piece of red skin. My lips are stained with wine, and I notice a slight vinegar smell falling out of my mouth. My teeth are most likely gray like they always get when I go top to bottom on a bottle. I am suddenly aware of how hot it is in the police station is and also suddenly aware that I am drunk, sitting in front of a police officer, trying to remember if I have ever known my license plate number. It turns out that I don't remember it, not even if it starts with a number or a letter.

The police officer is young, his small pale head carved into a crew cut. We continue to speak to each other as if he doesn't know that I am malfunctioning, that no one really stole my car. We also look at each other as he reviews the address on my driver's license and doesn't say anything about why I am driving when I live just five blocks away from the bars I had just come from. Oh yeah, I am driving because what was supposed to be a grocery run went off track and became meeting up with some friends for a quick lunchtime drink. But I can't have one drink.

The officer radios dispatch. He offers to drive me home, all half mile of a trip. They clear him to leave. We walk through subterranean hallways lit with the off-yellow meat of fluorescent light. My skin looks ill and bruised.

We leave the building, emerging into the basement level of the parking deck. A half dozen squad cars and an APC are parked here and there, spaced out like a lopsided chess game where all the opponent's pieces have been removed. We reach the officer's car. There is a bit of back and forth over the radio. We leave and enter the light of the afternoon sun.

All the windows are up in the squad car. I can clearly smell myself now. There is a bit more radioing, police talk that I can't pick up on. I am sure they are talking about me and my car in some manner, but it is so coded that it doesn't matter. Even I know the smell of a drunk. There is no way I left the station without anyone knowing it: it is the smell of cigarettes and laughter. It is the smell of stale and sticky lager nestled into the fabric weave of shoelaces and the cuffs of jeans. This officer knows these smells. He's stepped over and through them on sidewalks.

We turn right onto Market Street and make another right onto Second Street. In the shade of a live oak is my car. It is parked facing the wrong direction on the street. The officer parks his car, headlight to headlight, a first date. We get out; I stare at my hands as they shake and begin to blur.

Farthing Street was adapted from *Quitter #7*

Farthing Street

The weeds in the lawn are tall and heading out to seed, the view from our front stoop full of henbit, broadleaf plantain and pepperweed. The purple flowers of the henbit are easy to spot from any window in the house, forming a raised mat of contrast against a green understory. We haven't mowed in months, haven't bothered to pull the grasses from the mortared cracks of the brick stairs that descend from the street towards the slightly sunken house, haven't trimmed the waxy looking holly shrubs that edge the house. Because of this, the city of Durham has attached a large red and white cardboard placard to the small mailbox affixed to the house. The sign gives notice—in bold, uppercase letters—of an impending fine for homeowner's indolence, for creation of a public nuisance, and for failure to clear a lot.

I remove the notice and catch song sparrows in the act of building a nest in the mailbox. A clothespin attached to the lid to hold outgoing mail has provided just enough of a gap for the birds to get inside the box and go about their work. I open the lid to find twigs and very old leaves, brittle and translucent from months of exposure to wind, rain and sun. There is also dry green moss, pieces of polyester fluff and strands of fine bluegrass, all soft enough to eventually cradle the eggs underneath the exposed brood patch of the mother sparrow. In the right mood, I would view the nest as a beautiful creation. Instead I scoop all the material out and dump it behind the bushes that grow wild and crooked beneath the mailbox. I stick the clothespin in my pocket, go inside and lock the door behind me.

As I destroyed the nest, I realized I was losing my formerly intact sense of right and wrong. I am not myself in this moment. Or maybe it is better to say I am just a fraction of myself, a splinter of the person who had opened that same mailbox a few short weeks ago. Circumstances changed; I became a father, brought home a creature so delicate, so needy and demanding that it has become hard for me to maintain simple daily functioning, let alone keep up with consistent self-appraisal.

The lock clicks, and I set the notice on the end table. My body collapses onto the nearby couch. I stare into the translucence of the sheer window curtains in front of me and fade slowly into a daydream. At first I imagine myself as a plate glass window weakened by successions of thrown stones. I stop the stones from fully breaking me, but then I think about real windows and how it is only a matter of time before the glass cracks and slides against itself, falling forward into whatever it is the window defends against. The visions change rapidly, moving from the broken glass, to how the shapes of trees remind me of ancient fences, to a panic of thinking I have left my child in the car seat. I hear the sounds of the baby crying from the bedroom.

There is the newborn, the lack of sleep, the trauma of participating in a long and painful birth. Then there is the child's poor latch on its mother's breasts. I look at my reflection in the bathroom mirror. Despair saturates my face; anguish grows around my eyes, thick and sharp like steel wool. I catch myself staring into the spiral of a draining sink or lingering too long at the washing machine. I hold my hands on the corners as the old machine shakes through the spin cycle, the vibrations somehow reminding me of plowed soil, of the coldness of concrete, of impossibly blue skies. I want to be something else, somewhere else: I look out the door and see a plastic bag in the street, imagine the bag is the spirit of a great horned owl. It calls who cooks for you? Who cooks for you all? Why can't we be like birds, laying eggs and taking our turns incubating them, all the pain long gone before the first of our children emerge? Why can't we be like birds, short-lived and compelled by instinct?

I am not well, not well at all, and I think that there is not one thing I can do about it that makes the least bit of sense. Impulsively I open the closet door and look at the shotgun nestled quietly in the corner, the same shotgun I received as a present on my sixteenth birthday, the same shotgun I once used to shoot at deer and rabbits. I think about loading one single shell into that gun and going outside and just sitting down in the backyard under the sweet gum tree and sucking on that barrel like a steel-flavored Popsicle. I think about it, but I can't imagine my finger pulling the trigger. This isn't me; there is no way this could ever be me.

I have kept this gun clean and oiled for over twenty years, kept it out of sight and mentioned it only in passing as the birthday gift that it was. Kristin didn't care for it, but she also didn't care about it. As long as it wasn't mounted above the fireplace or trotted out for show-and-tell during potlucks, Kristin was fine with my keeping it. Five years after we first got together, Kristin and I bought a large piece of land in rural Chatham County, about an hour from where we live now. We envisioned creating a self-sustaining homestead, asking the soil and the forest for the things that we needed. When we lived on that piece of land, the gun had a purpose. It could be used against coyotes or dogs coming after the pigs and chickens, it could be used to shoot targets in the woods, and it could be used to hunt for food during the lean times. When we moved back to the city, its purpose became less certain and more imaginary.

"Let's be realistic here," Kristin said when I mentioned the gun's potential in robbery deterrence. *"You'll never get to the gun and then to the bullets in time if some fictional home invasion takes place. Just put one of our knives on the top of the dresser. If something ever happens, it will be better than nothing."* She's right; a knife is intuitive. Either of us could use it. She's pragmatic; the bullets – old target shells that, used in bad faith, would hurt and mangle but otherwise not be lethal – were stored too far away from the gun itself, a form of childproofing that rendered the gun useless for anything as unplanned as a robbery attempt. Kristin is not nostalgic for a time when my brother and I walked into autumn forests to make bird-shot scream into the leafless canopy, dropping dead squirrels to the crunching, wooded ground.

But still, looking at the gun and imagining what it could do is the darkest it can get for someone like me. This is one of those *"zero"* moments that a psychiatrist would later have me label on a calendar.

"If ten is the happiest you have ever been, when was your last ten?"

"I have never had a ten. What does that even feel like?"

"A ten would be a person's peak euphoria during the experience of something unique and special. It is a completely personal scale, not something that we all share. Does that make sense?"

"No. And I have never had a ten. I honestly don't know what that feels like."

"Alright. We'll come back to it. Do you know what day it is and where you are?"

It's hard to explain your depression to others, even therapists, who have never experienced the need to block out the sunlight with heavy curtains and remain still within that darkness. Depression can be like a frost: unpredictable, furious, disappointing. You hope it doesn't descend at a time that won't afford disruptions, a time of delicate growth.

I think about an image from a thin photo album kept amongst other artifacts at my father's house. In the photograph my father stands next to my stepmother. She is holding their small dog. They are both well dressed, standing there on her mother's back porch. She is smiling, he is not. A bandage covers most of his upper lip and a piece of his jaw. He still has stitches from a weeks'-old dog bite he suffered at a friend's house. I think they are dressed for Easter service, but I can't be sure.

In the image my father is thin, maybe the thinnest he ever was. He and my stepmother had been trying to conceive for years at that point, without success. I recognize myself there, recognize in his eyes that he is not mentally well, fighting something that he doesn't know how to speak about, maybe doesn't even know is something that can be talked about at all. He is suffering there on a porch, thirty years ago, in one of the smallest towns in Western New York. There are no facilities for him there, no helpful caregivers, no discussion of possible medications. For him there is only alcohol and wishes and too-short summer vacations with his children.

I see the way my father's eyes meet the camera, how his posture is frail and uncomposed. I looked the same when I set up a tripod and took photographs of myself and Tennessee in the first month of her life. A shadow lengthens from the photographs of the past and present, merging both fathers in ways that will not contract. Neither of us is truly there in those images.

I close my eyes and forget the photographs. I walk to the bedroom and reach for my screaming child.

*****

Kristin was twelve hours into labor when I fed her a small dollop of honey. Our midwives told me it would help to keep her strength up. She hadn't eaten since we had some cheap comfort food the night before. Her energy poured out of her in a summer sweat; I tried to capture it with towels as it seeped from her reclined body. She quickly vomited the honey along with some tea one of the midwives had her drink. Her vomit was green and frothy and smelled like recently turned compost. I was thankful that we had thought to line our mattress with a new shower curtain.

The smell of blood, feces and amniotic fluid created a thick and humid blanket around her. This barrier warped my perceptions, bent the light, muffled the sounds. I silently bothered myself with questions as I stifled my gags: *"Is this how this is supposed to work? Are we going about this correctly?"* "No," I answered. *"No, we are lost out here."*

The home birth process was a sick joke. We were naïve about childbirth in general—about the basic process itself—let alone how do go about it on the same bed we slept on every night. We did all these crunchy things we learned in birthing class—self-hypnosis, visualizations, nightly perineum stretching. *"The words,"* we called them, this thin bound notebook full of hypnotic mantras meant to make the whole process go smoothly and with minimal pain.

Kristin was nude. She had shed everything in an impossible pursuit of comfort. I could see her neck and chest muscles moving with her heartbeat. I imagined the pulsing umbilical cord inside her exchanging oxygen and carbon dioxide, swapping toxins for nutrition. Her skin was blotchy in spots where she had been rubbing against the bed covers. Her hair was wet from the washcloth I kept returning to her head, strands of her hair stuck to her face like tributaries on a geological map. All of her was beautiful and pure.

She shut her eyes tight. Her eyelids were pink with capillaries that I had never noticed before, a net holding in the visions she was unable to articulate in anything other than groans. I listened and watched and tried to think of what I would say to her the moment we'd first meet our child. Would it be something we would remember forever, a passing piece of knowledge so genuine and simple as to make all this time and pain seem like nothing? I hoped so.

2:00 AM – wake up, bloody show, contractions
:54 seconds, 3:50 apart. 3:30 AM first midwife arrives

This is the only record I managed to write down about the birth as it happened. I had wanted to document the whole process, scribble down all the little victories and write inspirational notes along the margins of the notebook. I had no idea that writing or even concentrating for very long would be impossible. All of my attention was focused on comforting the uncomfortable, forcing Kristin to drink water and breathe through the contractions. The midwives kept saying we were almost there.

"It won't be long now," they repeated as the moon came and went and came again. ***"We're almost done here."***

We stopped timing contractions sometime during the first day. Instead we all focused on getting the baby into the correct position to make everything work as nature intended. The midwives shifted Kristin around, made her walk and bend and get on all fours. They made her sit on the toilet for as long as she could bear it. We stood her up in the shower to spray hot water on her back. When she emerged pink and shaking, she would lie back down on the bed. The midwife would stick a hand inside her to try and move the rim of the cervix, asking Kristin to push against the pressure point of their fingers. She complied as best she could. The base of my guts fell apart each time they did this. I was sick with the feeling you get on the downward stretch of a roller coaster except this coaster had no bottom, just a constant drop at an unimaginable speed. Nothing was helping or working. The clock seemed to read hours and days instead of minutes and seconds.

When the midwife removed her gloved and bloodied hand it was always the same story—the baby was too crooked to let the cervix fully dilate. Her cervix was stuck at nine centimeters; Kristin pushed against what may as well have been the bolted door of a bank vault. *"Next time we'll get it. Rest for a bit, and we'll try it again."* Sometime during the second night they ran out of gloves.

"Say the words," she muttered from the start. I held the notebook close to my tired eyes and read slowly to her: *Drifting down, mind and body becoming more serene and peaceful…hypno-anesthesia becoming much more powerful now…Deeper and deeper now, that's good…* This went on for hours without progress or change. With the realization that the words were not helping, I felt old and useless.

Kristin became hoarse from a constant and primitive moaning. No matter which room I entered, my head was enveloped in the hum of her throat. Yet I could not leave her for more than a few minutes; the moans called me back as quickly as water spilling down a hill, eroding my ability to inhabit my own self and make decisions. Her pain was becoming my pain. All of our meticulous plans became hallucinations.

One of the midwives asked if we would consider leaving the house and going to the hospital; each of them promised they would stay with us and advocate for what was best for Kristin and the baby. It took little time to decide. *"Yes, let's go to the hospital. What do I need to do?"* We had not planned on going to the hospital. We were not prepared to go, and we were emotionally vulnerable to the idea. Kristin's greatest fear was being weak and talked into a Cesarean. She knew it was irrational, like her fear of snakes. We joked that she should feel sorry for snakes since they don't have any legs; we didn't have any such jokes about Cesareans.

While I packed a bag, I silently wondered: Were we going because the midwives had given up on Kristin and wanted their own involvement eased by the equipment of a hospital room? I buried my cynicism, moved quickly while the midwives got Kristin cleaned up. Slowly, they clothed her and helped her out of the house. She didn't speak, she just continued to moan.

*****

There is a blurry period between when we left the house and arrived at the hospital. One of the midwives drove Kristin. I drove our car with another midwife. I remember the drive was silent; we were not talking about the birth, the radio was off, the only sound was the occasional clearing of a throat. The white dashed lines of the highway passed by quickly, glowing in our headlights. They looked like the perforations of a massive notebook page that we were about to rip out. The rough draft was finished.

I parked the car and went to look for Kristin. I found her moaning in a wheelchair in the hospital lobby while one of the midwives negotiated the admission process. One midwife spoke to us about our options—epidural for pain management and sleep, Pitocin for controlling the contractions—all of which would be done under her guidance, as we were still technically in her care. OK, I told them. But we want the smallest amount of Pitocin as possible.

There wasn't much settling in the hospital room before there were machines hooked up and making their distinct noises. There was some back and forth about what was happening. Someone brought me coffee. The caffeine went in but never resurfaced. Kristin arched her back as the anesthesiologist inserted the epidural catheter. She was soon able to sleep. When she was comfortable, I stretched out on the vinyl couch under the windows and slept as well.

I awoke to noise and busyness. The room was full of people, most of their lower faces covered with masks. Someone calmly said the baby was crowning. The unmasked midwife quietly urged Kristin to push and breathe, push and breathe. By the time I knew what was going on and got to my feet, the head and one shoulder were on the way out. As I grabbed Kristin's hand, her final pushes brought the rest of the body out. There was an instant relief on her face. Our daughter was soon up on Kristin's chest, squirming and pink and alien. They were both very quiet. **"There are no bones in this one!"**, the midwife announced as the placenta came out. We were barely paying attention as she held up the organ to show off its deep red beauty, the afterbirth as an afterthought.

We took turns holding our daughter. She was quiet. The doctor and nurses packed up their equipment, signed off on documents. I stared at her, felt the softness of her skin, ran a trembling hand over the light hair on her head. We named her Tennessee Lynn and made plans to bring her home before another sun set. I could think of nothing memorable to say.

You and I cannot remember the day of our births. It is not possible or even desirable. We arrive in a foreign atmosphere, colder and drier than anything we have experienced. Our lungs inflate for the first time. We take a few quick pulls of air from this new planet and then cry out for a return to the liquid weightlessness we have come to know so closely. Fear is the first thing we know, a fear that is instinctual and unconscious. We scream out and make an announcement of our position to all the predators hiding nearby.

*****

I remember it was sometime in the fall of my junior year of high school; all day long the cool air dried my throat on its way in, the same air emerging warm and humid, personal clouds of breath falling up and away into the surrounding atmosphere. High school was in the small town of LeRoy in Western New York. The sky was gray, barely concealing the threat of snow or sleet. But it was too early for snow, even for this small town sandwiched between Lakes Ontario and Erie and its lake effects.

Fallen leaves blew into the street, crashing and skittering into each other like poorly made paper airplanes. Against that threatening gray sky the variant colors of leaves haloed the limbs of the nearly empty trees. Beginnings and endings are buried in this particular color contrast; browns and reds fidgeting against the dirty white background above us, those few final leaves holding on to that last stage of senescence just long enough to end up right on the top of the pile, the last to land, the last to decay.

What am I remembering exactly? It is the first time that I can—in hindsight—identify myself experiencing a period of depression. Sometimes I lay in bed for an entire day, stomach down, face toward the wall. I was immobile, pushed into the mattress by a compression of something outside of my control, something I did not understand. Breath came short and shallow, the room dark enough to give shadows very little running room into the corners. The sheets on the bed warmed rapidly and cooled slowly, crumpled in the middle and taut at the corners, stagnant under my weight and despite my darting thoughts. I felt like a leaf caught in the bushes.

When you are young, you can't assign a name to it, this thing, this depression. You think it is just a part of life, something that comes along with breathing and aging and carrying a heavy mammal brain. A decade or so in the future, visiting a psychiatrist for the first time, I learned that, left untreated, the first bout of depression will usually lead to another several years down the road. From there the half-life continues to decrease until a handful of minutes is all that stands between the dusk of one episode and the dawn of another.

At forty-one, I am old enough now that I no longer have horizons on which to seek shelter. It just comes on, a quickly spreading net of thoughts and inaction. There is no refuge, no chance to turn it back. It just comes.

There isn't anything particularly emotional about what I feel, just a low energy custody of hopelessness and sullenness, a cold thin soup of existence. My sighs become autonomic;

I chew my teeth and vibrate my fingers imperceptibly. I lose words, become silent as a conservation of energy, stare at things as if they hold me upright.

Having a new child magnifies all of this to levels I never thought could exist. Weeks after the birth, I searched for *"postpartum depression in fathers"* online. Casual reports indicate that one in ten men can be affected by postpartum depression during the first three months after birth. But according to a 2010 meta-analysis of medical studies, the Journal of American Medical Association found that this number surges to one in four during months three through six. And the risk of paternal postnatal depression increases in fathers who already have experience with depression.

But it is easy to miss this research. Before I found the JAMA study, I'd scanned medical websites related to postpartum or postnatal depression and found find little or no mention of men. In many of the journal articles I read, men were listed as a footnote, their depression offered as a symptom of dissatisfaction with marriage or with the baby itself. A man might be depressed because he wanted a boy but got a girl, because his wife is preoccupied with childcare, because sex is non-existent, or because there is no time to socialize, not because he has a stigmatized yet treatable disease.

There is no time to be sad, and if you are sad you are weak. That is how I felt. I became a ghost unsure of my manner of haunting.

*****

We kept the bedroom drapes shut tight for days. I used the darkness as a blanket. Tennessee would cry as I held her there in the room. She was so small yet so powerful, loud, her dark blue eyes wet under smooth eyelids. Even in the darkness I could see the tiny blood vessels in those almost translucent coverings. Was she wet or hungry or crying just because? Was she in pain? I told her I would feed her if I could, take her to where she needed to be if this room was too little or too big, if only she could just stop crying and tell me what I needed to do. I just needed someone, anyone, to tell me what to do.

At night, headlights passed over the thick curtains of the bedroom and sprayed glowing lines onto the far wall and ceiling. The light moved unevenly, and I imagined the noise the car tires were making on the warm, dry pavement. There is a rhythm to the street outside: the squeal of a loose alternator belt, pitch changes as gears shift down under a depressed gas pedal, bass lines escaping from old speakers. There is no quiet in the city. There are train horns and highways full of personal and professional freight. There are loud arguments and gun shots, sirens and laughter. I listened to Tennessee grunt and root as she lay on my chest.

I look back on the photographs of our new family and see my father's blank affect on my own face, a flatness in my appearance. I stare into my own eyes and remember how I yelled at Kristin, how I told her I couldn't do it anymore.

"What can't you do anymore?", she asked.

"Everything," I said, and that is exactly what I meant, that is exactly how vague I felt. My own skin and mind held nothing but a vapor.

I felt I could not participate in the raising of this child. I was done. I so desperately wanted out. I did not know what to do when the baby refused to latch on and eat. I'd never been so helpless, and I thought that by walking away from my family I could regain some order, some normalcy.

I thought about that gun in the closet almost every minute I was awake. It was in my vision even as I changed the diapers and made the lunches, heating up roast beef slices to take to the room I could barely stand to enter. Suicidal ideation is just what it sounds like. It is imagining ending your own life and imagining what other people's lives would be like without you.

Kristin and I looked at each other from across the bedroom. Ten years together and she knows when I am defeated. *"If the thought ever crosses your mind, you need to tell me,"* Kristin said, barely concealed fear beneath her delivery. *"You need to tell me."*

Her second sentence was the punctuation that brought me to silence; she rarely repeats herself. She sat on the bed holding the baby, and I stood slumped against the door frame, waiting for an opportunity to get the words out of my mouth: *"I have thought about it. I am thinking about it right now."* I couldn't tell her the full extent of what was going on with me. I could see no positive outcome from any discussion about harming myself. If I was going to pull out of this pit she had to know—or at least feel- that everything was going to be alright. I had to make it seem that recovery was coming. I told her that I was going to need help, that I needed her to help me. I told her I was weaker than she knew and that she had to see and accept that. Later that afternoon she gave me a list of mental health services in the area. I called and made an appointment for the next morning.

*****

We open the drapes and let the sunlight enter the room unfettered. My head is clear for the most part. I drape a blanket over the shotgun and do my best to forget about it. My anxiety softens to a whisper, and I accept that there are certain problems that are best addressed with mainstream solutions. Through several long weeks of intensive talk therapy, a nightly dose of 20 milligrams of escitalopram, and a morning dose of 150 milligrams of bupropion, I have opened myself up to a reprieve from this illness. This wasn't an instantaneous transformation, more like a bird hatching, methodically cracking pieces of the shell apart, expanding and stretching slowly as the big pieces fall away, realizing that the worst is over and it is bright outside.

Taking these steps was something that I knew had to happen but was unsure how to explain to Kristin or even to myself. The home birth, the aversion to medical intrusions: these beliefs did not exist in a vacuum. We eat pastured meat and know our farmers. We don't have a television. We use cloth diapers and dry them in the sun. I bike to work. Kristin planned to breast-feed until Tennessee turned two years old.

But: we use antibiotics as needed. We drink fluoridated tap water. Tennessee is up to date on vaccinations. We prefer the warm light of incandescent light bulbs.

We survive. From my previous experience with depression, I know that meditating and acupuncture and happy thoughts will not work. This illness is as much a part of me as my heart. I know that nothing other than pharmaceutical intervention will make me the person my family needs me to be. I will need to keep taking the drugs this time and accept that I may need them for the rest of my life. I explain to Kristin that just like she needed the support of a hospital to complete the birth, I need these prescriptions. It is not a weakness to accept this type of aid.

Now I mow the lawn when it needs it, chewing up all that henbit, knocking down the other weeds before they can spread. There is no malice, only a drive to keep things neat and trim and managed. One cool summer evening I mow while Tennessee stands framed within the screen of the front door, looking out and waving to me each time I pass. I can see her lips moving: ***"papa, papa."*** The sun falls lower as the smell of grass and gasoline spreads like ivy.

All I want to do is live.

Part Four:
Interviews

A Brain Map Q&A From Gut Feelings Zine

1. Do you actively do anything to keep your brain healthy, and if so what?

I read a lot. I also keep adding to my list of birds I can identify by song.

2. What or who mentally stimulates your growth the most?

I think watching my children discover things about themselves and seeing how they interact with the natural world are my main stimulants. The same is true as far as my writing is concerned; every memory I can harvest from childhood by watching and interacting with my own children is incredibly valuable. My whole style of writing is based on relating my past to my current life. That can only get deeper as the kids age.

3. If you could add or take away anything from your brain what would it be?

I would get rid of the pieces that control addiction, depression, and anxiety. I don't enjoy living with all of those parts, so I know I could live without them.

Frontal Lobe

4. Are you more emotion or reason based when making decisions?

Depending on the situation, I have become more of an emotional decision maker, mostly in the matters of people who have done me or my family wrong in some way. Otherwise I am very cautious and deliberate, churning my decisions over and over until I am about out of time to make that decision.

5. In what situations have you learned the most about yourself?

During the birth of my kids, after making the decision to move far from home, while replacing an alternator in my truck.

6. Do you think you have to learn good judgement? (Are people inherently self-destructive?)

I think we have to learn it to some degree, mainly through pushing our boundaries when we are very young. As kids we can watch how our decisions bring out reactions in the people around us and evolve accordingly. I can see it in my children. Personally, I think I am generally self-destructive, primarily because of addiction. I had to learn how to cope with the fact that I will always be an addict, I can't return to alcohol or whatever and expect that it would go well. I still haven't been able to write about it. I don't know how far away from it I need to be. But that is way off track from the question.

7. Do you have any daily or annual rituals? Are they personal to you or your family or are they related to your culture or religion?

Religion is not for me. We do not celebrate any holidays other than our birthdays. And Halloween. I do have rituals though – hug my partner and children every morning and evening, drink coffee every morning, take and post at least one photo a day (which I number) on Instagram. I also like to eat cereal or granola late at night.

8. If you could live inside of a book, which one would it be?

I would like to poke around in *The Left Hand of Darkness* for a bit.

9. Is it more important for you to speak or to be heard?

To be heard. I am not a talker, but I can write.

10. Do you think a time exists that is easiest to create? For instance, do you strike the muse or does the muse strike you?

I have to strike the muse. I work several very long days and late nights in a warehouse during the week. Our youngest child likes to get up at 5:30 in the morning after waking up several times in the night to breast-feed. Around the house, there is always something or someone that needs to be tended to. There just isn't enough time to sit down and focus on a sustained amount of writing. So I take whatever I can get. I write on my hand a lot. I have the Evernote app on my phone for quick notes, and I have notebooks everywhere so that I don't have to hunt for something to jot an idea or phrase down in. I think of things when I am in the shower and I have to rush to finish washing in order to get out to write it all down. Or I will be just about to fall asleep when something comes to me. I know I won't remember it in the morning, so I have to creep out of the bedroom at 2:00 a.m. without waking anyone up (the four of us sleep in one bedroom) to write myself a note. But a lot of the time when I could be writing or doing layout or messing around with photos, I just end up reading. It isn't a bad way to spend my bit of downtime, but there is a gnawing that I should be at least revising something I have written.

11. Do you have an emotional state that you find it easier to create in?

I have to be up for it. If I am in a trough of depression, I don't give a fuck about creating and don't give a fuck if I ever create anything ever again. I hate everything I have ever made. When I get out of the trough, I can get back to it and see the promise of creating again.

12. Do you think you have to have an elevated ego to be an artist?

I can see this either way. I think maybe folks see self-promotion as ego driven, but I see it more as survival. It goes back the question about being heard. On the other hand, if you are really working hard at your craft, then you are dealing with massive amounts of rejection and critique and people ignoring you. You need to have a durable ego to deal with that every day.

Parietal Lobe

13. What smells do you most associate with your childhood?

Cut grass, beer, cigarettes, plowed soil.

14. If you could only live on five ingredients for the rest of the life, what would they be?

Coffee, bread, peanut butter, almond vanilla granola, cheese.

15. Do you have a place you go to, either physically or mentally, where you feel the most at peace?

I go (mentally) to a very specific place in a very specific forest at a very specific time in my life. It is a massive downed beech tree that spanned a small stream in Pennsylvania called White Oak Run. The cabin I lived in was right there on the stream. It was 1997. I had just graduated from college in Western New York, moved to the coast of North Carolina (where I knew exactly one person), took a shit job ripping off old roofs of coal burning power plants, and just decided that I wanted to be an ornithologist. I applied to a bunch of birding gigs throughout the US and ended up working on a study of the Louisiana Waterthrush just south of Pittsburg. That job and that place have informed so much of my worldview and influenced so much of my writing that I can't believe that I was only there for four months. It was like I sucked that whole place into this dense piece of matter made out of solitude and bird-song and distance and stuck that piece of matter right where my guts connect with my rib cage. That is where I feel it and where I go.

16. *Do you think that people need some form of discomfort to make art?*

I think making art is uncomfortable to begin with. You are making something that you want others to connect with and understand on whatever level you want them to understand, and the odds of that happening are really slim. As far as the conventional forms of discomfort like poverty, substance abuse, bad breakups, depression, and all that, I can't really answer because I don't personally know the alternative. If I grew up rich and could have one drink and stop and have never been cheated on and had perfect brain chemicals, I'm not sure what my writing would look like or if I would even be driven to write. Living with or through discomfort gives me some amount of precision when I chose my words. It helps me make the reader really work for it no matter how much or how briefly it might hollow them out to do so.

17. *Are you more motivated by the promise of reward or the threat of punishment?*

Reward. And I need to do a much better job of practicing that in my day to day life, especially in my interactions with my kids.

18. How much does your conscience/morals come into play when making decisions?

I'm not a religious person, but I know I have a firm platform of personal morals and beliefs that I stand on. If you aren't at least subconsciously asking if a decision you are about to make is going to harm someone else, then maybe you shouldn't be in charge of making that decision. I'm looking at you cops and politicians.

19. Do you ever experience your emotions in physical ways? If so, how?

Depression makes me physically ill, like I swallowed rocks or glass and then got punched in the exact spot where that debris settled in my insides. It is exhausting as well. If I tell my partner I am not feeling well, they immediately know what I mean.

20. What is your least favorite physical sensation?

Being in the extremes of temperature. I hate shivering and I hate sweating just because it is hot out and not due to physical exertion.

Temporal Lobe

21. Do you think a person has to understand art in order to be able to appreciate it?

Yes and no. For example, I don't understand much about quantum mechanics, but I can appreciate everything behind the theories and applications. Understanding art can be a bit different. I don't think there is much to be objective about in art, just like an axiom is not made whole by subjectivity. That may bother the quantum philosophers of the world who believe that there is nothing that is not subjective, even calculus or physics, simply because everything in those fields comes from the observations of a single species. Or the art philosophers who believe that you must have objectivity to affirm subjective viewing of art. I find it hard to argue that the Second Law of Thermodynamics has any sort of subjectivity to it or that a person can view a Rothko or read Ursula LeGuin with cold objectivity.

22. What is your earliest memory?

Laying on a carpet, moving a small plate of some sort underneath a coffee table. My parents are there and the television is on.

23. Do you expect happiness in your life?

No, but I don't really expect anything in life except to be disappointed. That is pretty gloomy, but that is just how I see it. From growing up in an abusive home, I have to toil through my past (with the help of a therapist) in order to determine what it even means for me to be happy. I honestly do not know yet what it is supposed to feel like. That would be challenging, to expect happiness but not know, truly, what happiness is.

24. What flaws do you think you have when it comes to communicating with other people?

I am a horrible communicator. Everyone I work with can verify that. I don't usually enjoy talking outside of a ring of very specific people. I can do it, but it takes everything out of me. I also tend to bother people via e-mail or Facebook if I don't get an answer soon enough. I know that probably really fucking bugs them, but I can't help it. Once I get an idea in my head and someone else is part of it, I need my questions answered and I need them answered on whatever bizarre time frame I invent for myself.

25. What do you think your ex partners would say the hardest thing about loving you was?

Not knowing what I was thinking.

Occipital Lobe

26. What's the most unbelievable thing you've ever seen?

A baby being born. A Whip-poor-will's open mouth. A dumpster full of doughnuts. A barn roof full of vultures with their wings outstretched to dry in the sun.

A Conversation with Author and Publisher J David Osborne

JDO: *I checked out* Quitter *a few days ago, and when I first started reading it the main thing that jumped out to me right away was this kind of anti-holding-down-a-typical-nine-to-five-job attitude that I was getting. I was wondering where you were working when you quit this job that you hated so much, and what made you just finally say, "Fuck it"?*

Trace: I usually keep jobs for quite a while. I've actually been working since I was around 11 years old. My first job was picking strawberries for a roadside stand, but the job that I write about in that first *Quitter* is when I was an IT manager for a company that made laboratory equipment. I was doing that for about five years, but in my off-time I was making zines and participating in protests and living in a punk house, just being in the whole ideological and social anarchist world. The two didn't really line up that well; I kept the job because they had a really nice copy machine and I was scamming copies overnight.

Yeah, yeah.

But it got to be that it was really sucking the life out of me. I saved up as much as I could. I was living in a house with a bunch of other people and the rent was pretty cheap, so I made a go at not having a real job for a while. I made it about a year.

Was this job a lot of telling people to turn their computers on and then turn them back on again?

Yeah, it was a lot of that, but it was also taking computers apart and replacing parts and stuff like that.

That's actually kind of fun, though. That's actually working with your hands, so...

Yeah, it was—it was alright. It wasn't really something I wanted to do, and I didn't want to keep up with the technology. That was another problem. As the technology developed and evolved, I didn't, and I reached a point where I did not want to know about it anymore. It was not interesting to me. I mean, it wasn't all that interesting to me to begin with, but it paid well.

It's interesting how soothing a balm a good paycheck can be. You know what I mean? It can keep you doing shit that you really don't want to do because you're like, "Well, I like to eat and I like to pay my rent". When you quit, did you feel terrified or were you pretty high on it?

I was relieved. Because I knew that being particularly resourceful with finding food or finding different little mini-jobs would not be a problem for me just to keep going. I survived off my savings for quite a while before I had to do anything that brought in money.

Yeah, that was going to be my next question was how you made it a whole year without having to work.

A lot of dumpster diving, a lot of just living cheaply, biking everywhere. It's really formed the rest of my years after that. I mean, that was quite a long time ago.

How so?

Just being scrappy and learning to live with less.

I guess you've always kind of been scrappy, I think you mentioned that.

I got scrappier before I took that year.

What's picking strawberries like? Tell me about picking strawberries.

As an 11-year-old it's intense because you're trying to pick all these berries for this roadside stand that is very busy. It's a couple other 11-year-old kids and an 18-year-old telling you what to do. It gives you the work dynamic pretty early on.

So, you understood middle management right away. That 18-year-old, that was middle management right there.

Yeah, for sure.

I don't think middle management ever really grows up past that age, right?

Yeah. They're always taller than you and telling you what to do. I had a lot of those kinds of jobs when I was growing up.

I did the strawberries for a couple summers and then went to work on a cabbage farm. That was way more intense. Very, very long hours, hot and humid and it was just relentless.

Was it just the quantity that you had to pick, or was there something particular about it?

It was the whole process. I started off doing this thing called "planting skips", which is when you walk behind the machine and put transplants in all the gaps that the machine missed. So, you're just walking all day through these massive fields.

And I'm assuming it's hot as hell?

Yeah, and from that you graduate to riding on the machine, which means you're slapping a transplant in every second. It's all stuff that you get used to, but then you move on to the next thing and you don't think you're going to get used to that, then you do, and it's just more life skills.

Have you had a job that you particularly enjoyed?

I like my job now, and I liked my job after my year off. I started working in a food co-op and became the produce manager there, and then I worked for a farmer-owned wholesale organic produce distributor. I've been there for over eight years now. It's the longest I've ever had a job, and I particularly like it.

Do you have any kind of overall philosophies about what white-collar jobs are doing to our psyche as a people? Are you kind of anti-them in general or do you think maybe that they're sort of okay for some folks?

I think some people maybe are born for it, and it's—I don't know, I'm just not sure how many more of those folks can be that our economy can hold on to, since we're moving to more automation and service-type jobs. I'm just not sure how many more accountants there can be in the world.

Well, hold on, I guess I kind of feel that way about writers sometimes, too. I'm like, "Jesus, how many more—," but I guess what I'm saying is that writers as a sort of profession, you know, because it seems like there might be kind of a scarcity with that. What do you think?

With being a writer as a, like a successful writer?

Whatever that means...

Well, I mean if it's meeting your needs and your goals, then I would consider that successful.

I would agree with that, sure. I've been looking a lot at this basic income thing, and that seems like a pretty sweet idea to me. Of course, whenever I tell some people about that, they're like, "Well, if you just give everybody ten thousand dollars a year, nobody's going to do anything," which is just not true, right. To my mind, if I had an extra ten thousand dollars a year I'd be able to do more of what I do anyway, because I wouldn't have to do bullshit to just make sure that ends meet.

Yeah, because over the timeline of a year, ten thousand is not a whole lot that you could consider doing nothing all year...

Right, right, exactly.

It would be an addition to whatever other money you're hustling up.

So, what made you decide to start the zine in the first place?

I had gone to visit an old college friend and just saw how they were living, and how I was living and how it was completely disconnected. They were living in this immaculate town-house with everything provided for them as far as lawn care, and all the homes looked the same. I decided that that wasn't the kind of progressive that I wanted to be. That was where his politics were, the regular white-collar democrat or whatever you want to call them, and it was at odds with what I saw that I wanted to be part of. I didn't want to destroy a swamp to put up townhouses and then replant a constructed wetland. It didn't make any sense to me. So, that's where a lot of writing the original issue came from. It was supposed to be a one-off thing for my housemates, and then pass a couple around. I never really thought about it going anywhere. I can't read it now. It's not particularly well done.

I disagree, sir. I disagree. I liked it very much.

I wrote that in 2005.

Right, yeah, I don't think I look at things that I wrote in 2005 either. I think 2010 is my cut off.

Yeah, I mean that whole book, *Good Luck Not Dying*, it cuts off at 2011, and I think that I've progressed way beyond that since then.

One thing that you mentioned that I wanted to talk about that you reminded me of is when you said that you'd gone to your buddy's house and this was a progressive person, right? Like liberal democrat kind of thing. What's so interesting is I grew up in Oklahoma pretty much my whole life, and that's one of the reddest states in the entire United States, and the whole time you're there you think to yourself, "Man, if I could just get out of here and live amongst people who think the way that I think," right? And then a few years ago I moved to Portland, which is a very blue city. I moved here and what shocked me was that, the people still aren't particularly nice. They don't really seem to give a shit about anything. I thought I was moving to some sort of like liberal paradise, but it just turned out that liberal people are just a different kind of asshole than conservative people, but they're kind of just all assholes. That's my misanthrope message for the day.

Being nice does not qualify you for being either liberal or conservative, I'm afraid. Being nice seems rare in general.

Yeah, because you still have, like you said—I mean, it seems like where I come from in Oklahoma, the typical asshole ideas that you don't care about anybody else, you just take care of yourself, who cares, get a big truck, slap some truck nuts on it, this cowboy hat, everything else, and then you move up here and it's like buy organic, have a bunch of coexist bumper stickers, but you're still driving a car, you're still buying a massively expensive condo where somebody's home used to be, because there's this rapid process of gentrification. And so it seems like they're both really self-satisfied with themselves. But I think that in a way maybe the liberal end is even worse because they deluded themselves into thinking that they're good, whereas the conservatives that I know at least, take pride in proudly not giving a shit.

There is some self-satisfaction, but I think if you want to get beyond that and be a liberal—liberal or progressive—then you need to embrace a little bit of hypocrisy. I drive a truck. There are no truck nuts on it. It's not particularly big, it's a little Nissan truck. I used to have a big stack of Nader/LaDuke bumper stickers that I would put on my vehicles way after the elections, just to see if there would ever be any reaction. Never really, nothing really happened.

Yeah, I've never seen people get mad about bumper stickers, but I don't know. I've never put a bumper sticker on my car just because—well, because I mean in Oklahoma, that's actually where somebody would get mad at you for having a certain kind of bumper sticker.

I grew up in Western New York. It's a rural place, and it's probably exactly like Oklahoma. I think rural America is similar everywhere.

Right, and it's interesting because in moving to Oregon and visiting cities in general, you find out that as soon as you drive maybe ten, fifteen minutes outside of the city you're right back ideologically where you started, if you come from a place like Oklahoma.

It's not far away, that's for sure.

So, you moved to Durham. How are you liking that? I visited your fine city about a year ago and I loved it.

Durham is definitely one of those bubble cities that, I don't know. I love Durham; it's really awesome. It just has a lot going on for it, but it's also starting to be built up in a way that people are not reacting too well. There's a lot of gentrification going on and myself and my family we're partly to blame for that. We're a white family living in a historically black neighborhood, and there's a lot of empty houses around us. They're getting bought up and then flipped and sold for way more than they're worth. That's pretty much a vehicle for displacement of the population that had lived here before. There's the argument that, well, no one else is buying the houses so wouldn't you rather have someone living in that house than have it to be vacant? I would say, "yes" but I don't want it to be turned into a really expensive rental either.

Yeah, it's hard to figure out how to fix because it seems like it's happening everywhere. It's already completely happened to San Francisco, Portland, Seattle. Are you a particularly politically-minded person or could you really just not really care one way or the other?

I still carry my anarchist politics around, but I do vote and I know a lot of anarchists that vote. It's not that—you don't have to adopt the whole platform, I guess.

I'm kind of ignorant about anarchists—what exactly do you mean by that?

Mutual aid and direct democracy and everybody being involved in the decision-making process. Also an individual knowing what is best for them and trying to live a life that does not impact people in a negative way.

Right.

So, that's the basics of it, and also trying to either break down or reform the structures that tower over us that have no accountability to people. So, it's really micro-democracy in a way.

I wanted to talk about Quitter 10 *which is your new zine.*

Yeah, it's the latest. I'm really happy with that one.

Yeah, because it covers to my mind a few different themes but all works together as one big piece. It definitely all flows together. Do you want to set the ground work for what it's about and then I can ask my very pointed, excellent Charlie Rose-esque questions?

It's about shedding institutional memory especially from a family perspective. If something disappears—I think I talk about the house that my grandparents had that the fire department burned down as practice, and now that house and everyone who lived there has no significance to my kids. And if I were to explain it to them, would they care, do they need to care? It's a lot about that, and current memories and about how we're trying to raise our children. I'm not sure that there's an actual overarching theme other than memory.

I think you pretty much nailed it. You have a couple moments there in particular when you're a kid and you're going to, I believe it's your great grandad's funeral, and you talk about how you didn't really care. There are a few scenes in there that really resonated with me because they touch on how you never really seem to be able to under-

stand how to act when somebody dies. This year has been pretty crazy on my end of things because a lot of people just started dropping dead very suddenly. And I had been relatively sheltered up to this point, and then it all hit in one fell swoop. It was bizarre because when they got sick, I said, "Well, at least they're still alive. I mean, they're sick, but they're still alive," and then as soon as they died, and these were people who were close to me, I thought, "Well, they're dead now. There's nothing I can do about it." You know what I mean? But you never hit that sweet spot where you feel like you're really accepting it or coming to terms with it, I guess. I don't know. It's a weird thing but that really resonated with me.

I was seven or eight when my great-grandfather died. I was four when my paternal grandmother died, and then it wasn't until I was going to college that my paternal grandfather died. I don't really have anything in my recent past. I had a grandfather that I was fairly close with before I moved to North Carolina and he died in 2008, somewhere around there. So, that's the most recent. I also talk about my partner's miscarriage in this issue, and that's one that is not necessarily something that you can get over very quickly or at all. That's very personal. It's not a detached grandparent or parent; it's really close. So, I think that's the kind of the contrast that I wanted to put in there. I hoped that that comes through.

It did. You know, honestly, I didn't necessarily connect that but now that you say it, it makes a lot of sense that there is this kind of difference between them. There's that with information as well. The idea of what information is important to pass on to kids is really important too, because you have a segment in there where you talk about this hat. And

I thought that was a really good example of what's actually important for you to pass on to your kids.

Exactly. It's hard to know, but I know that the hat is one of those things because it's never going to mean anything to them.

Right, but you do make some sort of suggestions because you talk about your mother and how she won't talk about what happened between her and your dad. Are you suggesting that just admitting mistakes is important? What were you getting at with that?

It's having her come to terms with what it meant to me and my brother. I talk about the divorce being the fracture that made me who I am, basically. That was a pretty big deal when you're five years old that your parents are no longer going to be together. And there's always going to be this other place, this other "who", this other thing that could have been. I think that acknowledging that that had a huge effect on me and my brother. We've both gone on to suffer from depression, we're both recovering alcoholics—we both have these issues that I'm pretty sure came from that split. And then my mother marrying an abusive man after my dad, definitely did not help. So, it's admitting that this had some really physical and emotional impact on your children. I think it's important for me that these things be acknowledged and not just saying, "Oh, that was forty years ago, get over it," because that's not happening.

Right. I think that I have a similar thing except for me it's with my dad. He seems to have created an entire world for himself about what happened during those years. And

I'll talk to him and he'll say, "Do you remember this, this and this," and I'll be like, "That's a completely—," like, he's constructed a whole story, basically. So, to him, I don't even know if getting the truth would be possible at this point because he's built up so many layers to it.

Is this about a divorce, too?

Oh, yeah, absolutely. Anytime I do something that's kind of fucked up I remind myself of my dad and it freaks me out. In a sense he's been a good role model in reverse.

What not to do.

There did seem to be another thing that you seemed really intent on communicating knowledge about nature. There's a lot of instances where you talk about birds in this. You want to unpack that for me, what that was doing?

I've always been interested in birds. I did a research project on birds in a forest for three months a long time ago. I think I write about it in the book about studying particular birds, but as far as the nature bit, I really want to pass that on to my kids. I see how interested my daughter, Tennessee, is especially with wild edibles and identifying bird calls that it just makes me want to keep learning myself. I like birds in general for their imagery. You can use them for a lot in writing, and I'm trying to get better at that. They're all over the place in my writing.

Yeah, it does feel like a lot of the sections start off with trees and birds and things like that. You definitely have that nature vibe going on which I dig.

Yeah, I've been called a scruffy nature writer.

Why scruffy? What's up with that?

Well, it's not straight up nature; it's using nature as the character, basically. It's not writing about "Oh well the tree has eight leaves and they're all opposite"—

Dude, I'm hooked. Sounds good. You just got your first sentence of your next zine.

I wanted to mention real quick that a lot of these pieces that are in *Quitter 10* have been developed into their own essays, and that essay—the part about my grandfather's hat and the divorce, I recently won a creative nonfiction award from the North Carolina Literary Review. I was pretty happy that that could come out of a zine. I have all these other pieces that I'm working on. I'm working on the one about the horse chestnut tree and there's a lot more to that story, and the miscarriage, there's a whole lot more to that.

Why aren't you supposed to lick your fingers after you touch the seeds of a chestnut tree?

They're poisonous if you eat them. That's really all I know. As far as licking your fingers, it might be good, might be bad. I don't know. That's why I ask the question: Would you lick your fingers?

Right, right, right. And so for the hat and the divorce thing, I'd be really interested to read the more extended essay version of that because it is kind of interesting. Do you think, let's say hypothetically, you're in your mother's position and you have fucked up badly and you've hurt your family for it: do you think that you'd be able to sit down and say "Here's exactly what happened"? Just to lay it out on the table to kind of clear the air in a sense?

I think that I would definitely owe it to my children for them to understand. I mean, we don't hold anything back from them now. I don't see how I could possibly do that knowing my own life and my own situation and how much I would really want to know the answers to, "What happened? What went wrong? Why is this how we now have to live our life?". I would have to tell them exactly what happened. It would need to be age appropriate.

Sure, absolutely.

It would be an evolving conversation, and they would have new questions as they grow older and have their own interactions with other people. So, yeah, that's my answer. I'm not planning to do that by the way. I have no intent—

Well, no. This is a total hypothetical, just getting a little insight there. I wanted to talk about this new book.

I consider *Quitter 6* to be cutoff point for me to where I actually started to take it seriously, the writing. Up until that point it was just a hobby, just an idea to put stuff together once in a while and send it out and just see what happened. But with *Quitter 7*, I sent it off to a bunch of distributors to see if they could pick it up, which is something I hadn't done before. Jessie Duke at Pioneers Press wrote back sometime later and said, "Yeah, we'd love to get this in." So, that was the point where it took on a much bigger life than it had. So, now there's hundreds of copies of just that one zine out there.

What made the switch for you? What made you decide to go big with it?

I think because someone actually took it seriously and said, "This is good stuff. We want to work with you. We want to see you do more." So with each new issue it's still the same style, it's still the same voice but I'm taking more time with it and I'm developing more of a running theme that people can pick out in each issue. And I'm writing for an audience now, not just myself, so that's why I kind of take it a little bit more seriously.

Right on. So, with All I Want To Do Is Live *which is this new compilation, it's going to be limited, right? It's a limited run of books?*

Well, it's going to be a lot bigger initial run. Since I have so many personal connections with readers, I wanted them to have this nice-looking book to go along with what's inside of it. I don't think I could put myself through churning out a generic, glossy book. A lot of the reason that this book is what it is is that we were thinking that we were going to reprint my first anthology *Good Luck Not Dying* because there's only a thousand copies of those, and I was really hesitant to make that available in that amount again. I like that it's going to end, it's going to sell out and then that will be it. The *Good Luck Not Dying* era is complete. I can move on to something new and different. So, we were going to reprint it with *Quitter* 1 through 10 and then add in some extras and the more and more I thought about it I just didn't want to. The stuff from *Quitter* 7 and on is not really part of *Good Luck Not Dying*; it's something different. I just wanted to take it in a different direction. I love designing my own zines and such, so going in that direction was also something that is fulfilling to me, to do all the guts and the cover on my own.

I have one more question and that is what if ten years down the road, you have this impulse to put these old **Quitters** *out again, do you have to stick to your guns there and say, "No, that was a period in time. It's over. No more," or are you kind of easy on yourself with that rule?*

I would probably be easy on myself, but I don't know. I don't know. Ten years from now, who knows what I'll be doing.

Yeah, it's true.

Who knows what I'll be writing.

*****

Thanks!

The following people contributed to the campaign to print this book

Amy Eller
Bancha Srikacha
Luke Hirst
Andrea Wood
Jessica McMains
Collier Reeves
Elizabeth Friend
Patricia Daggett
Maggie Morgan
Heather Davis
Melissa Bell
Kathleen Moss
Camille Armantrout
Laura Cloak
Crystal Dreisbach
Vanessa Oniboni
Oliver Luker
Maryah Smith

Jenny Schnaak
Jess Kemp
Jill Trufant
Alison Rudel
Debbie Roos
Alexis Luckey
Emma Burn
Mathew West
Walter Martens
Sandi Kronick
Tanis Clark
Kurt Morris
Leanne Simon
Hannah Spector
Laura Grant
Logan Mock-Bunting
Carol Hewitt
Lauren Atherton

Kim Lan Grout
Kate DeMayo
Colleen Kendrick
Maya Ribault
Ariel Greenwood
Ashley Betters
Joe Jones
Tristin Miller
Elizabeth Reed
Robert Mulvihill
John Bonitz
Beth Johnson
Laura Friederich
Shelly DeAntonio
Sophia Ioannou
Paul Finkel
Lisa Ramsden
Richard Baiocco
Salem Neff
Kaitlyn Dennehy
Ginnie Hench
Donna Spruijt-Metz
DL Anderson
Leonora Tisdale
Shawna Kenney
Nina Bar-Giora
April Chase
Michelle Moll
Jillian Johnson
Kamara Thomas
Jonathan Farmer
Judith Jones
Brandon Hines

Steven Horton
Anthony Garguilo
Libertie Valance
Catherine Elander
Angelina Koulizakis
Lisa Sorg
Christel Cothran
Alix Blair
Jack Finn
Amanda Sand
Liz McGuffey
Elisabeth Effron
Christopher Tonelli
Vicki Lofquist
Vanessa Hernandez
Javier Pacheco
Andrew Wiles
Emily Bischof
Laurel Ferejohn
Jaime Kozlowski
Melissa Norton
Alyssa Bicoy
Laura Mindlin
Lindsay Perry
Christina Askounis
Elaine Bleakney
Tyler Jenkins
Frank Overton
Jessica Wadleigh
China Medel
Stephanie Schlessman
Karen Saludo
Rann Bar-On

Tal Matalon
Anna Lee
Brandi Perri
Kelley Bennett
Adrien Lopez
Amber Bishop
Ross White
Michael Belleme
Hope Wilder
Heather Bixler
Angie Raines
Hannah Shumaker
Stephanie Stewart
Sugar Island Bakery
Paul Finkel
Rhiannon Fionn-Bowman
Sonya Cheney
Mitra Sticklen
Ramon Gil
Olivia Mertz
Grace Glasson
Melanie Gardner
Jonas Cannon
Ana Owusu-Tyo
Valerie Fann
Naomi Swinton
Sam Hummel
Chris Jude
Stephanie Woodbeck
Jessica Freeman
Laura Stephenson
Alice Osborn
Jamie Beck

Paul Sampson
Mary Roche
Andy Myers
Dalice Malice
Harry Albert
Sarah Wagner
Jazz McGinnis
Alan Swart
Karla Capacetti
Alisha Mullin
Jūs Percy
Alyssa August
Andrea Stewart
April Matos
Jeremy Levine
Kimberly Schwartz
Laura Grant
Mark Herbert
Nicole Accordino
Ted Conover
Suzie Kelly
Carey Reynolds
Kyle Harris
Amy Godfrey
Abby Nardo
Deb Taft
Hope Sutton
Dylan Patterson
Stewart Fuell
Morgan Capps
Kathryn Waple
Chris Lott
Amber Greune

Dakota Floyd
Keith Kincaid
Kym Register
Brooke Shuman
Ellen Bush
Cameron Goodyear
Renee Gaudet
River Takada-Capel
Jessica Hogan
Casey Landau
Brittany Sweeney
Wanda Sundermann
David Thornton
Elise Rocks
Frank Hyman
Derek Rowe
Judas Bardon
Alexor Moore
Phoebe Lawless
Tiffany Salter
Abigail Smith
Chris Stevens
Alex Adams
Caroline Hanner
Cea Flowers
Matt and Dana Rudolf
Dayna Meyer
Nathaniel Klein
Raymond Goodman
Samantha Overmyer
Vimala Rajendran
Lynn Casper
Stephanie Deady

Shaena Mallett
Patricia Adams
Blake Hocker
Dayna Sterlachini
April McGreger
Susie Newberry
Jolie Day
David Osborne
Annita Sawyer
Jill Reemsnyder
Laura del Castillo
Jane Kelly
Flower Conroy
Crystal Dreisbach
Antonia Crane
Zachary Black
Joellen Craft
Anita Koester
Tanner Postma
Mikel Barton
Patricia Daggett
Sonya Johnson
William Hooper
Jennifer Wyn
Monika Gross
Emma Burn
Shawna Sheely-Redding
Gareth Strange
Alissa Brandemuhl
Tracy Kondracki
Neal Curran
Jeremy Staples
Richard Baiocco

Bart Schaneman
Jennifer Curtis
Eileen Ramos
Paul Mirek
Veronica Thompson
Jane Kelly
Greg Lindquist
Wendy Crim
Amanda Dale

Gary Stevens
Sean Hart
Mark Gravel
Mary Feddeman
Ruth Berger
Jessica Bausemer

Additional Thanks

Kristin, Hazel & Tennessee
Elizabeth Thompson
Adam Gnade
Jessie Duke
Pioneers Press
Belle Boggs
Duncan Murrel
Bread Loaf Writers' Conference
Firestorm Books
Asheville Zine Fest
Zine Machine Durham
Regulator Books
Bibliopathologist

Lasterday Press
The Change
Queenfin.com
Abraham Ramirez
Hatchfund
Gut Feelings Zine
Fábio Vermelho
Sweater Mouth
St. Anthony
Rust Belt Jessie
Amy Eller
Schezelle Fleming
J. David Osborne

Also by Trace Ramsey -
Good Luck Not Dying

WWW.TRACERAMSEY.COM

About the Author

Trace Ramsey is a recipient of the 2015 Ella Fountain Pratt Emerging Artists Award in Literature, a 2015 contributor in non-fiction at the Bread Loaf Writers' Conference, and winner of the 2016 Alex Albright Creative Nonfiction Prize from the North Carolina Literary Review. Trace lives in Durham, N.C., with his partner and two children.

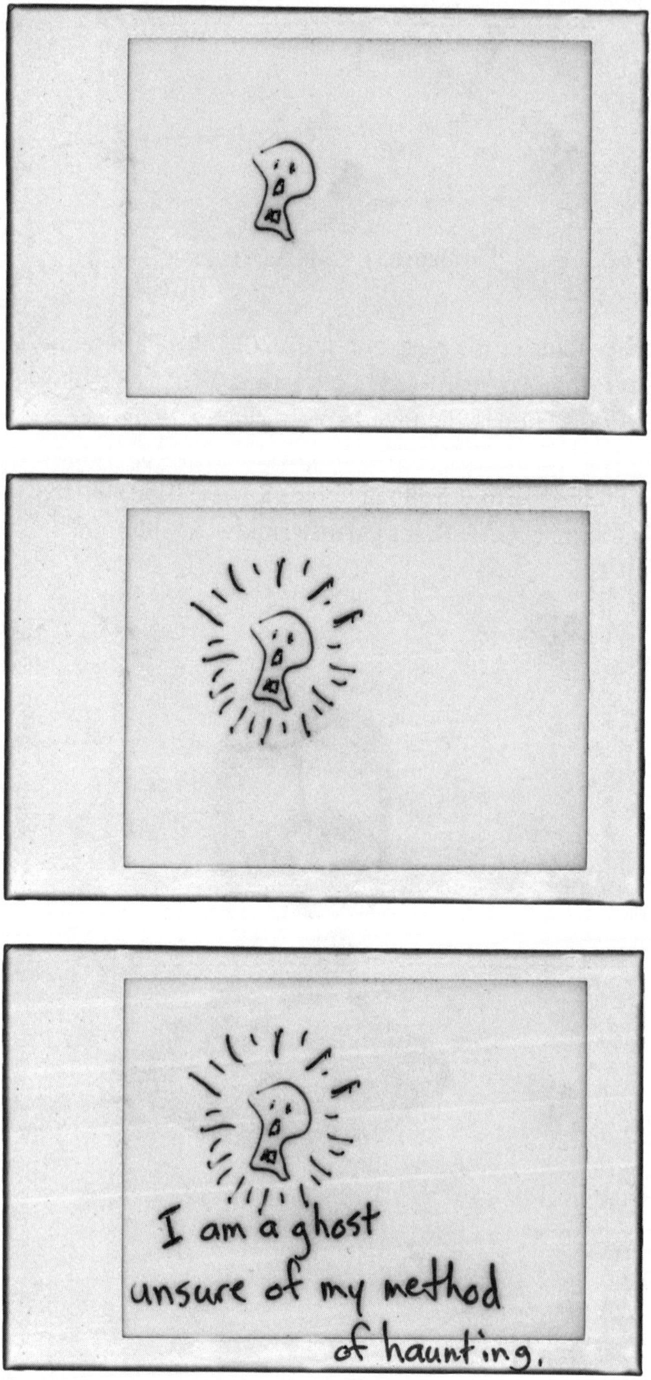